The Deity of Christ

By Frank Bartleman
This Edition Edited by Anthony Uyl

Devoted Publishing

Woodstock, Ontario, Canada 2017

The Deity of Christ

By Frank Bartleman (1871-1935)

What Think Ye of Christ?
Is He God or Man?

This Edition Edited by Anthony Uyl

The text of The Deity of Christ is all in the Public Domain. The cover and background art, layout and Devoted Publishing logo are Copyright ©2017 Devoted Publishing. This edition is published by Devoted Publishing a division of 2165467 Ontario Inc.

What kind of philosophies do you have?
Let us know!

Visit our online store: www.devotedpublishing.com
Contact us at: devotedpub@hotmail.com
Visit us on Facebook: @DevotedPublishing

Published in Woodstock, Ontario, Canada 2017

For bulk educational rates, please contact us at the above email address.

ISBN: 978-1-77356-152-3

Table of Contents

INTRODUCTION

This little volume has been prayerfully collected and written to meet the oncoming, terrible onslaught against, and the denial of the absolute Deity of our Lord Jesus Christ, in these last, evil days of apostasy from the true and living faith.

It might be truthfully titled forty volumes in one, for it is the condensed testimony and teaching of a vast number of the very best Christian scholars, dating from the early church fathers down to the present day, on this most important and vital subject of our Christian faith. In fact it contains the very essence of Christian belief concerning the doctrine of the Godhead, both from a theological and a Scriptural standpoint.

It is a book especially to be recommended as of helpful value to scholars, and in fact to all who desire a clearer- understanding of this most sacred and profound subject. May the faith of many be built up, strengthened, and restored through its perusal, is the sincere prayer of its author and compiler.

FRANK BARTLEMAN
Los Angeles, California
March, 1926

CHAPTER I

In attempting to write on this lofty and sacred subject we are well aware of the danger of "fools rushing in where angels fear to tread." Some one has truly said, "In mysteries men soon lose their way." Men become confounded when they seek to fathom the being of God.

By the help of God we will "let the lid stay on the Ark," - (1 Sam'l 6:19), not seeking personally to pry into things unlawful. In fact the major part of our task will consist of quoting what others far more able have had to say upon this subject. We trust the reader may derive as much profit from this study as the writer has. If so he will feel justified in having written.

If there are any people on earth who ought to welcome such information it is the Pentecostal people, for whom we more especially write. We are free from party spirit. The fact is many of us are becoming Higher Critics, and downright Modernists, on this subject. We are in grave danger of lining up with the Antichrist in the Apostasy. Anything that opposes or rejects a full Scriptural revelation of Jesus Christ must be antichrist. Because some have gone "beyond the things which are written," (I Cor. 4 :6, II John 9, R. V.), is no excuse for us to be frightened back and deny our Lord. Let our sympathies be placed on the side of right always. God will hold us accountable for this failure. Many have denied today truths once held through fear of being numbered "among the transgressors." "Art thou also of Galilee?" This is ever the devil's master stroke. He will push a people over the precipice, frightening the others back too far, one extreme always producing another. Jesus is thus again "crucified between two thieves." Let us come up to the help of the Lord. Both are robbing Him of the glory due Him. The one by unscriptural extremes, the other through cowardly denial of their Lord. Though one extreme may hold the other in subjection for the time.

Men are naturally creatures of extremes, on all subjects. And the truth is most generally found about the middle, in between. It is also hard to be shown anything in the heat of battle. There is the smoke of conflict in our eyes. It is hard for a sectarian to believe that anyone can really be free from selfish, party spirit. But we want the balanced truth, free from preference or prejudice. Extremes divide. They can only hope to meet in the middle, in Christ. The Sun sometimes appears oblong at the time of rising, through refraction of its rays. But it is the Sun nevertheless. So truth regarding a subject does not always appear clearly in the beginning.

We have this treasure "in earthen vessels." Crude ore is not gold bullion. It is easier to burn a man at the stake than to answer his arguments. Ignorance and prejudice are the greatest enemies of truth.

We need far more than a Sunday School or Kindergarten revelation of Jesus today to enable us to triumph over the Antichrist, the Beast and the False Prophet. "Unto a full grown man, unto the measure of the stature of the fulness of Christ." - Eph.4:13 "A spirit of wisdom and revelation in the knowledge of Him." - Eph. 1:17. Any true Christian must rejoice in the discovery of all revelation that tends to bring their Lord more powerfully and fully before their vision. We only know God by revelation.

It has been often said, and truly, that men are willing to make Christ "a little more than man, but a little less than God." But this can never be. He is either creature or Creator. If creature, we may not worship him. All great truths of the Bible run through the whole Book. They are never dependent or founded on some isolated Scripture.

Our first study will be that of the subject of the Godhead. This we will consider both from the standpoint of theology and Scripture. Tradition is so binding upon the consciences of most believers that the matter needs to be clarified for simple minds as far as possible.

As Christians we are called, according to the tenets of our faith, to walk a path between two extremes of unorthodox opinion. That is, between the idea of God as a mere. Monad, or a oneness as a single human individual is one, and the pagan idea of "gods many," or that of three separate Gods. This latter is known as Tritheism. The fact is, as generally accepted by all orthodox believers, God is neither one as man is One, nor three, as men are three. The truth lies between these two conceptions. God is a trinity of being, a three-one God, a tri-part Being. The Germans call it' the "dreieinigkeit" (threeoneness).

We might as well admit a most patent fact to begin with, that the Godhead has no human analogy. To this all scholars agree. The human mind can never "by searching find out God." Men are seeking on all sides to understand and explain the being of God through human reasoning and analogy. This cannot be done. God is not "such an one as we." - (Psa. 50:21.) "God is Spirit."

The declaration of the doctrine of the Swiss and German Protestants (Zwingle and Luther), reads as follows: - "We believe that this same God, one in essence and in nature, is threefold in person, that is to say, Father, Son, and Holy Ghost, as was declared in the Nicene Council, and as all the Christian church professes." While the word for God in Genesis is plural, yet this certainly cannot denote three Golds, for the very genius of the Christian faith lies in the fact of there being but one true God, one Supreme Being, one "first cause." "Hear, O Israel; the Lord our God is one Lord." - Deut. 6:4. There have been none added since. God has no beginning. Eternity knows neither beginning nor end. Only time and finite nature begins and ends. This one true God is tripartite in nature and manifestation. He ever existed as Father, Son (Logos, the Word, more properly expressed), and Holy Ghost. There are three eternal distinctions in the Substance of God. But, "these three are one." - 1 John 5:7. The Logos and the Son are one.

Wm. Smith, L.L.D., in his Bible Dict., a book all scholars are familiar with as a text-book, states on this subject: - "The plural form of Jehovah (Gen. 1:26), has given rise to much discussion. The fanciful idea that it referred to the Trinity of Persons in the Godhead hardly finds now a supporter among scholars. It is either what grammarians call the plural of majesty (pluralis excellentiae'), or it denotes the fulness of divine strength, the sum of the powers displayed by God." The old Swedish monarchs titled themselves in the plural as individuals, after this idea. The late Kaiser of Germany signed himself "Wir, Wilhelm, von Gottes Gnaden," - (We, William, by the grace of God). However, this does not in any sense affect the truth of the Godhead.

Dr. Scofield writes: - "The Supreme Being is One but, in some sense not fully revealed in the O. T., is a unity in plurality. This is shown by the plural name, Elohim, by the use of the plural pronoun in the interrelation of Deity as evidenced in Gen. 1:26, etc. That this plurality is really a Trinity is intimated in the three primary names of Deity. God, in His own triune Person, no human being in the flesh has seen. But God, veiled in angelic form, and especially as incarnate in Jesus Christ, has been seen by men."

No orthodox Christian or scholar has ever believed in three Gods, or in three separate Supreme Beings. That there can be but one Supreme Being, one first cause, is a fact attested to by all Christian scholarship in all the world, in all ages. God is one, and the Word of God is one. That the Jehovah of the O. T., is the' Jesus of the N. T., is also attested to by all orthodox scholars, such as Dr. Scofleld, Dr. Torrey, Adam Clarke, etc. And this really goes without saying, for the Logos (Word), is God's "thought and expression," in the very meaning of the term. The thought and expression in the O. T. and the N. T. are one and the same, the revelation cumulative. It is all the Word of God, the thought and expression of the one God. "In the beginning was the Word, the Word was with God, and God was the Word" (Greek). - John 1:1. German and Spanish translations read the same. God was never a non-entity, a mere blank, without thought or expression. His "thought and expression" (Logos) are a part of His very self, of His Being, begotten of Him. Just as my thought and expression are inseparable from myself.

Dr. Adam Clarke, the "Prince of Commentators," has the following to say: - "In all transactions between God and man, mentioned in the sacred writings, we see one uniform agency.

The Great Mediator in all, and through all, God ever coming to man by him, and man having access to God through him. This was, is, and ever will be the economy of grace." "There is one mediator between God and men, himself man, Christ Jesus." (I Tim. 2:5) "The lamb slain from the foundation of the world." Rev. 13:8. Provision has been made for every possible contingency before it could arrive.

Clarke comments on the following Scriptures: - Gen. 12:7 "The Lord appeared unto Abraham." This was probably by the great Angel of the Covenant, Jesus the Christ.

Gen. 12:8, - "And called upon the name of the Lord." Abram was taught even in those early times to approach God through a Mediator; and that' Mediator, since manifested in the flesh, was known by the name of Jehovah.

Gen. 16:7-10 - "The angel of the Lord." This was Jesus Christ who in a body suited to the dignity of his nature frequently appeared to the patriarchs. Also Gen 18:22. Of God the father, no man hath at any time seen His shape (Deut. 4:12-16), nor has He ever limited Himself to any definite personal appearance.

Gen. 22:11 - "The angel of the Lord." The Lord Jesus, who called himself Jehovah (Vs. 15, 16). "Swore by Himself," Jehovah (Jesus). - Heb. 6:13-18.

Gen. 32:24 - "There wrestled a man with him" This was the doubtless the Lord Jesus Christ, who among the patriarchs, assumed that human form, which in the fullness of time he really took of a woman. (This was only a form at this time, possibly vaporous or gaseous, compact to visibility which could be dissipated in an instant. I have given the sense of the comment on this point, to save space.) He could produce the effect on Jacob's body to appear a real man wrestling with him.

Jacob's wrestling was also spiritual. V. 30, "I have seen God face to face," - the Lord-Jesus Christ. (Of course we know the human nature and body of Jesus did not exist until formed and produced in the womb of Mary. Otherwise his conception, incarnation and birth would necessarily have been a farce.)

Gen. 35:13 - "God went up from him," visibly. This was no doubt the future Savior, the Angel of the Covenant.

Gen. 48:16 - "The angel which redeemed me from all evil." The Messenger, the Redeemer. We have full proof that this was no created angel, but the Messenger of the Divine Counsel, the Lord Jesus Christ. (The word angel means messenger' also. Not necessarily of the order of created angels Rev. 2:1.)

Ex. 4:2 - "The angel of the Lord." Not a created angel certainly, for he is called Jehovah (V. 4, etc.), and has the most expressive attributes of the Godhead applied to him (V. 14, etc) Yet he is an angel, a messenger, in whom was the name of God (Chap. 23:21), and in whom dwelt all the fullness of the Godhead bodily (Col. 2:9), and who, in all these primitive times, was the messenger of the covenant - Mal. 3:1. And who was this but Jesus the Leader, Redeemer and Savior of Mankind?" - Dr Adam Clarke. The Jehovah of the O. T. is proven to be the Jesus of the N. T. He is the Word or Memra, later made flesh, and dwelt among us.

The Chaldee Paraphrasts, the most ancient Jewish writers extant, use the word Memra, which signifies the Word, in those places where Moses puts the name Jehovah. These writers ascribe to Memra (the Word), all the attributes of Deity. They say it was Memra, or the Word, which created the world, appeared to Moses on Mt. Sinai and gave him the Law, speaking to him face to face. Which brought Israel out of Egypt, marching before the people, and wrought all the miracles recorded in the Book of Exodus. The same Memra at Bethel, appeared unto Abraham in the plain of Mamre, and was seen of Jacob to whom Jacob made his vow, and acknowledged him as God. - Gen. 28:20." - Alexander Cruden.

It is said of Augustine that one day walking by the seaside deeply engrossed in thought and meditation over the mystery of the Godhead, he observed a little child dipping the water out of the sea into a shallow hole he had just formed in the sand. Upon being asked why he did this he replied that he intended to put the sea into that hole. The conviction came powerfully upon Augustine that he was attempting precisely as impossible a thing in seeking to comprehend and explain mystery of the Three in One.

Some one has truthfully said "The infinite truth of the Godhead lies far beyond the boundaries of logic, which deals only with finite truths and categories." But the revelation of it is in the face of Jesus Christ," according to the Word. - 2 Cor. 4:6. The Logos (Word), the pre-existent Christ, is one with God. "In the beginning was the Word." - John 1:1. It was already there. God exists from eternity, throughout all eternity. "From everlasting to everlasting thou art God." - Psa. 90:2. No orthodox scholar ever taught that the Logos or Word had a beginning in eternity. In fact eternity knows no beginning. "In the beginning" predicates a starting point to reason from. Or it simply states the fact that "in the beginning" the Word was already there. The Logos is without beginning or end. In fact He is "the Alpha and the Omega the beginning and the end." - Rev. 18:17. A beginning without beginning "And God was the Word." - John 1:1.

Jesus Christ, the Son of God, is in His Deity of necessity as uncreated as God Himself. Were it otherwise He could not be Deity. Deity is uncreated, without beginning or ending. Deity is one inseparable of necessity in life and attributes. Hence all scholars declare that God the Son has the same attributes as God the Father, differing in office only, as Son, neither existing before the other.

Alexander Cruden in his Concordance gives to the Son of God the following titles in the Word which accredit him with the attributes of God. "Ancient of Days, Creator, Emmanuel, Eternal Life, Everlasting Father, Father of Eternity, First and Last God, Most High, Jah, Jehovah, Living God, Strong God, Mighty God, etc., etc.," In fact if Jesus were not absolute Deity we would have no right to worship him. He must be God. "Worship God." = Rev. 19:10. Cruden also says: "The Son of God is equal and consubstantial with the Father. He is, the express image of the Father, as our words are of our thoughts. - John 1:3; Heb. 1:3; 11:3.

Jesus Christ is not a created being, not a creature, but Creator. "All things were made by him." - John 1:3. To declare him less than absolute Deity is to make him a creature. To say he is divine, but not Deity, means nothing. A long tailed coat and a piece of parchment, or a roll of sermons, makes a modern divine.' Divinity is Deity or it is nothing. "God the Father, God the Son, and Got the Holy Ghost," are equally God. All this orthodox scholars have always taught.

A difficulty has been raised over the term "begotten," as applied to the Son. But all scholars' agree that the Son, or Logos, could not have had a beginning in eternity. He could not be "co-eternal with the Father," and have a beginning. From standpoint of manifestation as the Son, and as to his human nature, He had a beginning, from the womb of Mary. But in His Deity he was uncreated, as all scholars teach and declare. Many do not seem to realize they have an Eternal Lord, in the person of Jesus Christ. He is more than a Sunday School or Kindergarten Christ, more than a mere human sacrifice, yes, more than a Son even. He is both the Son of God, and God, according to all orthodox theologians. He is both the pre-existent Logos, which "was God," and the Son of God.

The Logos proceeded, or came forth, from God. - John 8:42. "The only begotten Son, which is in the bosom of the Father, he hath declared him" - John 1:18. This has reference to his coming into the world. The Son, and the Logos, the Word, are one. He was the Logos, (thought and expression of God, in the bosom of the Father, before he was manifested as the Son, of God. In His Deity He was always in heaven, omnipresent.

Tertullian wrote, A. D. 200: - "The Word (Logos) was sent from the Father into the Virgin, and was born of her, both Man and God, the Son of God, and called Jesus Christ.

Theologians have sometimes applied the term begotten' the pre-existent Christ, or the Logos, as though He were begotten from eternity, or eternally begotten, but this they have never implied as a beginning of existence. They all claim the Logos is eternal. The Word is begotten, as my thought and expression are begotten of me. They are a very part of myself. No less, and of as long duration. This is what theologians mean by the Logos, or Son, being eternally begotten,' or "from an eternity begotten of the Father." Some claim a continuous begetting.

In Acts 13:33, Paul refers the Scripture, "Thou art my son; this day have I begotten thee," to the resurrection of Christ. - (Psa. 2:7). "This day," in time. There is no time in eternity. (Heb. 5:5.) Read Rev. 1:5, Rom. 1:4, Heb. 1:5,6. - Compare Luke 2:13, 14, John 1:14, in parenthesis. John 1:18; 3:16-18, I John 4:9, John 17:18, Luke 1:35, "begotten." - Rotherham. Gal. 4:4. In Rev. 1:5, Heb. 1:6, the word is properly born,' not begotten. The Logos was sent into the world through the incarnation, as a Son, clothed in humanity. Heb. 1:2, I John 4:14, John 1:1 John 3:16. "A child is born, a son is given," - Isa. 9:6, as every child is born, and son given. Though in this case Jesus was Deity, the Logos. Only his humanity was "begotten" in the womb of Mary. "And God was the Word (Logos)." - John 1:1.

The Word (Logos) was sent into the womb of Mary and "became flesh." (the only begotten from the Father. - John 1:14), The Incarnation took place. A Son was manifest in Bethlehem's stable. The pre-existent Word abode forever. The Son revealed the Fatherhood. God was never known as Father until the advent of the Son into the world. The Jews never knew Him as such.

Jesus and the Logos are one and the same. Leon Tucker has said: "The Word of God and the Son of God are eternal and inseparable." "Therefore also that holy thing which shall be begotten' of thee shall be called the Son of God." - Luke 1:35, - Rotherham. "Thou shalt call his name Jesus." - Matt. 1:21, 1 John 4:15. "God sent forth his Son, born of a woman." Gal. 4:4. "Hath in these last days spoken unto us in the Son." - Heb. 1:1-2. The "Word of the Lord" (Logos) came to the prophets. "There are three that bear record in heaven, the Father, the Word, and the Holy Ghost: and these three are one." - 1 John 5:7.

Dr. Adam Clarke, the "Prince of Commentators," co-worker with John Wesley, has written the following interesting matter on this subject: "They have taken away my Eternal Lord, and I know not where they have laid him.

"I believe in the Holy Trinity; in three persons in the Godhead, of which none is before or after another. I believe Jehovah, Jesus, the holy Ghost, to be one infinite eternal Godhead, subsisting ineffably in Three Persons; I believe Jesus Christ to be, as to his divine nature, as unoriginated and eternal as Jehovah Himself; and, with the Holy Ghost, to be one infinite Godhead, neither Person being created, begotten, nor proceeding, more than another. As to its essence, but, one Trinity, in an infinite, eternal and inseparable unity; and this triune God is the Object of my faith, my adoration, and my confidence. But I believe not in an eternal sonship or generation of the Divine nature of Jesus Christ. Here, I have long stood; here I now stand; and here I trust to stand in the hour of death, in the day of judgment; and to all eternity. (One can readily judge how strong were Clarke's convictions on this point.)

"The doctrine of the eternal Sonship of Christ is absolutely irreconcilable to reason, and contrary to itself. Eternity is that which has had no beginning, nor stands in reference to time; Son supposes time, generation, and father; and time also antecedent to such generation. Therefore the conjunction of these two terms; Son and eternity, is absolutely impossible, as they imply essentially different and opposite ideas. (Poetry and human sentiment notwithstanding.)

His human nature is derived from the blessed Virgin Mary through the creative energy of the Holy Ghost; but His Divine Nature because God, infinite and eternal, is uncreated, underived and unbegotten; which, were it otherwise, He could not be God in any proper sense of the word; but as He is God, the doctrine of the eternal Sonship must be false." - Adam Clarke.

Clarke admits a three-fold personality, or three persons, in the being of God from eternity, but rejects the idea of Sonship before the advent of Jesus in the flesh. Before that He was the Word or Logos (John 1:1-14), the idea of sonship being transferred back to the Logos. A multitude of spiritual leaders of the church today agree with Clarke. Critics in referring to this particular view of

Adam Clarke have been content to pass it over with the simple observation that "this opinion has not been generally accepted." The Logos and the Son are one.

The Son is evidently in no sense inferior to the Father in His Deity, except in office. Deity is Deity. He was "equal with the Father." - Phil. 2:6, but "emptied himself," becoming inferior only in his humanity, through the Incarnation. Nothing has ever been added to or taken from God. Deity is self-existent, uncreated. Are not then the theological expressions "begotten from eternity," or "eternally begotten," as applied to Christ, mere technical human terms, their meaning in this connection understood only by scholars? They agree that these are not intended to postulate a beginning for God the Son, nor any increase, or inferiority in Deity. The Son of God was "begotten", humanly speaking, in the womb of Mary. - John 3:16. Before this He existed eternally as the Logos. He is both "God the Son," and the Son of God.

W. H. Bennett, a well-known English writer, has said: - He (Christ) became (in the Incarnation), what He before was not, but He did not cease to be what He was, - (very God)." All orthodox scholars declare the Christ to be not only the Son of God, but "very God." "Very God and very man." In fact they declare Him to be as much to God as God the Father is superior in office only. This is an accepted tenent of orthodox theology. All scholars admit there is no human analogy whererwith to express or define the matter of the Godhead. They admit that the Logos or Word is without beginning, even as the Father; and that the Word of God and the Son of God are one. The real, scriptural, mystery of the Godhead lies in the Incarnation. God manifest in the flesh." - 1 Tim. 3:16.

The well known theological expression, found in the so-called Athanasian Creed, "Neither confounding the Persons nor dividing the Substance (Essence)," we consider a safe proposition. Granted that the Substance or Essence of the Godhead cannot be divided or separated, it becomes impossible to make three separate Persons or Supreme Beings out of the proposition. Hence we are saved from Tritheism, the postulation of three Gods; to which Trinitarianism is admitted by scholars to come dangerously near. As the whole-question hinges on the use of the word "Persons," it might prove helpful to look more carefully into the meaning of this much argued term, as used and purposed originally in this connection.

In Nelson's Encyclopedia we read: - "It is generally conceded that the Christians of the second, and even of the third century, were far from having a clearly understood and recognized doctrine on this high subject (the Trinity). At the council of Nice, A. D. 325, they began to formulate a creed on this order. But the doctrine of a Trinity of Persons was not fully complete till the addition of the Filioque clause in the Western Church of the 6th Century, which led to the separation of the Greek church from the Latin. A declaration of the nature of the Trinity was finally draw up to meet certain heretical declarations regarding the same matter."

Philip Schaff, D. D, L.L. D., writes: - "God is one in three persons or hypostases (subsistences - used by Greek theologians to denote each of the three subdivisions of the Godhead; Latin personae,' from whence comes our modern term persons applied to the Godhead), each expressing the whole fullness of the Godhead. - (Col. 2:9, 10.)

"The term persona is taken neither in the old sense of a mere personation or form of manifestation (face, mask), nor in the modern sense of an independent, separate being or individual, but in a sense which lies between these two conceptions, and thus avoids Sabellianism on the one hand, and Tri-theism on the other.

"In modern philosophical usage the term person means separate and distinct rational individual. But the tri-personality of God is not a numerical or essential trinity of three beings (like Abraham, Isaac and Jacob), for this would be tritheism; nor is it, on the other hand merely a three-fold aspect and mode of manifestation, in the Sabellian or Sweden-borgian sense, but it is a real objective and eternal, though ineffable distinction in the one Divine being, with a corresponding three-fold revelation of this being in the works of creation, redemption and sanctification.

"In the Trinity there is no priority or posteriority of time, superiority or inferiority of rank, but the three persons are coeternal and coequal."

In the Dictionary of the. Apostolic Church, by Jas. Hastings, D. D., we read: - "The technical terms by which the christian church has expressed the faith that it derived from the Scriptures were not invented for a considerable time after the Apostolic period. Thus no one would expect to find the terms Trinity and Person in the N. T. The word "Trinity" referred to God, was first used by Theophilus of Antioch, A. D., 180. But it was not then an accepted technical term. Theophilus did not use the word "Trinity" in the technical sense in which it was even later used. The words which we render "Person" are of a still later date, and at first exhibited a remarkable fluidity of signification, being at one time used to denote what is common to the Father, Son and Holy Ghost, the Divine "Substance," and at another time to distinguish between them.

"The student must necessarily be always on his guard against the supposition that "Person' means individual', as when we say that three men are three persons. These technical expressions are but methods of denoting the teaching found in the N. T. that there are distinctions in the Godhead, and that while God is "One" yet he is not a mere Monad. These technical terms are not found in the Apostolic or sub-apostolic writings.

"It must be remembered that human language is limited and unable to express fully the divine mysteries, so that just as the technical terms, "Trinity," "Person," may be misused in the interest of Tritheism, so subordination (of Son and Spirit) may be misused in the interest of Arianism (a supreme God and two inferior deities)."

J. Munro Gibson, M. A.: D. D., writes: "The word Trinity" does not occur in the scripture, nor is there anything to be found there corresponding to those complicated formulas by which theologians have tried to define the relations of Father, Son and Holy Ghost. If theologians had only followed, the Scriptures in this respect, how many bitter controversies might have been spared, and how many needless difficulties and perplexities would have been avoided."

Dr. Scofield, in his Reference Bible, write as follows: "The name of God (El, Elah, Elohim) suggests certain attributes of Deity, as strength, etc., rather than His essential being. God subsists in a personality which is three-fold, indicated by relationship as Father and Son: by a mode of being as Spirit: and by the different parts taken by the Godhead in manifestation and in the work of redemption - Spirit, Father, Son." A tri-personality.

"Calvin did not enforce the Athanasian Creed, and did not use the words Trinity and Person in the confession drawn up by himself and others at Geneva." - Encyclopedia Britt.

CHAPTER II

Pastor Andrew Fraser of Chicago has written: "It is in the writings of Theophilus, bishop of Antioch, toward the close of the second century, that the term "Trinity" occurs for the first time, though other writers ascribe the coining of the term to Tertullian. In this case the pen was mightier than the sword, judging by the degree of strife its use has occasioned.

The Athanasian Creed in its definition of the trinity is such as to cause some minds to sacrifice the Trinity to the Unity, while others sacrifice the Unity to the Trinity, and thus lead the mind into a doctrine of three gods, or tritheism. The one God exists as the Father, the Son, and the Holy Ghost, and in some inexplicable manner the three interpenetrate each other and form but one being.

"We are fully aware of the custom obtaining among the Hebrews of using the plural term where we would generally use the singular. But since we believe in the presidency of the Holy Spirit in the task of revealing God to men, it is not difficult to believe that the use of the plural "Elohim" has behind it inscrutable wisdom looking toward a future unfolding of the truth regarding the Trinity.

"It is most unfortunate that in a discussion of so important a character we should find ourselves obliged to use words which fail to express adequately the ideas; and words which the Scriptures themselves do not employ. We are confronted with such a difficulty in the use of the word "Persons." Since the Scripture themselves nowhere use the word, the Athanasian Creed in its attempt to suppress the Sabellian heresy went somewhat beyond the simplicity of the Bible by the introduction of the term. When we remember that there is no case exactly parallel to the relationship of the Trinity, then we understand, that necessity has not yet coined the proper word.

"We cannot separate the Father, Son and Holy Ghost into three distinct personalities as we do in the case of three human beings. We must beware of ascribing to the tri-unity of the Godhead human form and human characteristics or attributes. Would "Subsistences" prove any more satisfactory for this idea? By subsistence or substance we mean "essential nature." Subsistences are not separations, yet they would admit of distinctions in a Being who is purely spiritual.

If we were to affirm a separate and distinct Divine Intelligence operating in each of the three "Persons" of the Godhead then we would have three Gods. We know that divine nature is one. For the sake of executing the Redemptive plan, the subsistences or substance resolved itself into a tri-personal Being in the forms of Father, Son and Holy Ghost Communion with God is not with one solitary monotheistic.

Editor R. E. McAllister has written: "We readily admit that when we express ourselves by saying "Three Persons in the Godhead" we are using terms not scripturally correct. Everything in the Godhead is prompted and executed by one personality. God is not a unit as a human being is one, neither is He three as three human beings are three. The three-fold relationship of Father, Son and Spirit is the prominent feature of the N. T. This relationship is vital and essentially necessary to a right understanding of the atonement and mediation of Jesus Christ.

"God has not seen fit to explain to reason the mode of His existence in detail as a basis for doctrinal discussion. We are met with an insurmountable difficulty when we undertake a philosophical explanation of Infinite Being in the form of finite thought and physical comparison. That there are three identities in relation in the mode of God's existence, Scripturally termed Father, Son and Spirit, no one would deny, but that these three identities can be properly called distinct personalities in the absolute sense of the word we question.

"The terms "Person" and "Persons" are never used in Scripture with reference to God. Heb. 1:3, R. V. - "Substance." God is infinite and eternal. Earthly limitations forbid a comparison of God's likeness that would be explanatory. Infinite being is characterized by attributes such as Omniscience, Omnipotence and Omnipresence. Deut. 6:4, "Hear O Israel, the Lord our God is one Lord," is a compound unity. Man was made in the intellectual and moral likeness of God without reference to corporeal form. Col. 3:10, Eph. 4:23, 24. It is as inconsistent to take a stand for one Person in the Godhead as it is to take a stand that there are three Persons. God is essentially One and manifestly Three."

Editor E. N. Bell wrote as follows: "No well informed intelligent Christian holds that there are three material bodies in the Godhead. Thousands of simple, unlearned saints think of God as a great big, mighty man sitting on a material throne in heaven, but mature and properly informed Christians know that this is error. Even that of Jesus which was corporeal was not Deity, but human. While the Father and the Spirit each have a distinct identity of their own, yet apart from the body of Jesus neither has a corporeal or material body. Jesus is the only person in the Godhead who has such a body, - a spiritual body.

"There are no other three in all the universe so related as Father, Son and Holy Spirit. There is no use to look among men for a complete analogy. They could not exist separated in essence, and could not exist independently of each other without being three gods. As seen by the human eye or mind they appear as distinct persons, yet behind the screen on the eternal side they are united in one nature, one essence one life, one existence.

"God is a being who is not limited by the confines of a single personality. That Father, Son and Holy Ghost are distinct, is an unquestionable fact, but that they are separate as individuals are in the natural, or that they are in any sense independent of one another, is not at all true. Herein lies the mystery. God is not corporeal, nor material, but spiritual in His nature or being. The Spirit has no fixed form or may be manifested under any form or symbol which it pleases God to manifest. The nature of the Father, Son and Holy Spirit is one, their essence is one, their being is one, their essence is one, their being is one, their existence is one. Each is uncreated and eternal, each is Deity, each is God, yet not three Deities, not three Gods."

From "Binney's Compend," used as a text-book in most theological schools, we gather the following: "The Trinity is indeed a mystery, and must necessarily remain so to us. Its incomprehensibility, however, proves nothing but that we are finite beings, and not God. The Sun is three in one. Round orb, light, heat. Man is three in one. Soul, rational mind, body. Three persons in the Godhead, though distinct, are separate. The Son and the Spirit proceed from the Father, yet they are of the same duration. The same attributes and acts, in the Scriptures, are ascribed to each of them without distinction. (Then follows a list of Scriptures, are ascribed to each of them without distinction. (Then follows a list of Scriptures proving this assertion.) In a word, all divine operations are attributed to the three. - 1 Cor. 12:6, Col. 3:11."

Augustine taught that "the Father and the Son are the one principle of the Being of the Spirit." - John 10:30, 1 Tim. 3:16.

Dr. Isaac Barrow defines the subject of the Godhead as follows: "The sacred Trinity may be considered either as it is in itself wrapt up in inexplicable folds of mystery, or as it hath discovered itself operating in wonderful methods of grace towards us. As it is in itself it is an object too bright and dazzling for our weak eye to fasten upon, an abyss too deep for our short reason to fathom.

"There is one Divine nature or Essence, incomprehensibly united, and ineffably distinguished, a communication without any deprivation or diminution in the communication, an eternal generation, and an eternal procession, without any division or multiplication of essence." Deity is neither increased nor diminished. Nothing has ever been added to or taken from Deity.

The Nicene Creed, A. D. 325 reads as follows: "The only begotten Son of God, of one substance with the Father. But those who say: There was a time when he was not; or the Son of God is created; they are condemned by the holy catholic and apostolic church."

The Athanasian Creed reads: "We worship one God in Trinity, and Trinity in unity; neither confounding the Persons, nor dividing the Substance. The Godhood of the Father, of the Son and of the Holy Ghost is all one, the glory equal, the majesty co-eternal. Such as the Father is, such is the Son, and such is the Holy Ghost. The Father eternal; the Son eternal; and the Holy Ghost eternal. And yet they are not three but one eternal. So likewise the Father is Almighty; the Son is Almighty; and the Holy Ghost Almighty. And yet they are not three Almighties, but one Almighty. The Father is God; the Son is God; and the Holy Ghost is God. And yet they are not three Gods; but one God. And in this Trinity none is afore, or after another; none is greater or less than another, but co-eternal and co-equal.

"Our Lord Jesus Christ the Son of God, is God and man. Perfect God and perfect man. Equal to the Father as touching his Godhead." From the Nicene and Athanasian Creeds, the early church doctrine of the Trinity is principally formed.

Agreement of Bonn, 1875: "In the Godhead there is only one beginning, one cause, by which all that is in the Godhead is produced." ("I and the Father are one." - John 10:30.)

The Confession of the Greek Patriarch, Gennadius to Mahomet II, read as follows: "We believe that there are in the one God three peculiarities, and these three peculiarities we call the three subsistences. We believe that out of the nature of God. spring the Word and the Spirit, as from the fire the light and the heat. These three, the Mind, the Word, and the Spirit, are one God, as in the one soul of man there is the mind, the rational word, and the rational will, and yet these three are as to essence one soul." This was the faith of the Greek church at this date. 1453, A. D.

From the Catechism of the Greek Church, Moscow, 1839, we gather the following: "The Son of God begotten of the Father expresses that personal property by which he is distinguished from the Father and the Holy Ghost. None should think that there ever was a time when he was not." Jesus, the Word, was "in the bosom of the Father," His "thought and expression" (Logos), from all eternity.

"Light of lights" explains the incomprehensible generation of the Son of God from the Father. Both the light we see and the Sun axe of one indivisible nature. "Very God of very God." The Son of God is called God in the same proper sense as God the Father. - 1 John 5:20. (There is no increase in Deity in this so-called "generation.")

"Jesus suffered and died not in his Godhead, but in his manhood. The Son of God is omnipresent. In his Godhead he ever was and is in heaven. He is omnipresent, on earth and in heaven. He became visible in his humanity. He was always in heaven and on earth. His humanity had a beginning.

"How does Jesus sit at the right hand of God the Father? This must be understood spiritually. Jesus Christ has one and the same majesty and glory with God the Father. God's special presence is manifested in heaven to blessed spirits; also in the church a spiritual presence in various manifestations, gifts, etc. But "God is Spirit," omnipresent.

"How does Scripture ascribe to God bodily parts, as heart, Eyes, ears, hands, if God is a Spirit? Holy Scripture suits itself to the common language of men; but we are to understand such expressions in a higher and spiritual sense.

"The Son of God was made man, without ceasing to be God. The "Word was made flesh." - John 1:14. One Person, God and man together, a God-man." - Greek Catechism.

I. M. Haldeman, D. D., Pastor of the First Baptist Church, New York City: "God, the one being, is expressed in three persons. No one person is God without the other two. The Father can neither be seen nor felt; the Spirit can never be seen, but is felt; while the Son can be both seen and felt. The Son of God is the revelation of both the Father and the Spirit, therefore the embodiment of the fulness of God. - Col. 2:9, 2 Cor. 3:17. Father, Son and Holy Spirit constitute one being and one God.

"God is ever essentially the same. The being of the Father would not be complete without the being of the Son. The Son of God is the outgoing and forthputting of the essence and energy of the Father. "Whose goings forth have been from of old, from everlasting." - Micah 5:2. He never in all eternity was unbegotten. He is the uncaused Son of God, and God the Son.

"From all eternity He has been a common part of the being and substance of God. Since this his true His mother could not conceive His personality. Therefore that which was conceived by his mother was not a personality, but an impersonal nature. "That holy thing which shall be born of thee shall be called the Son, of God. - Luke 1:35. "Wherefore also that which is to be begotten' " - Luke 1:35, Rotherham Translation. "A body hast Thou prepared for me." - Heb. 10:5 (His human nature was begotten" in the womb of the Virgin.) His body (the expression of his created human nature) was united to His unchanged personality. While the Holy Ghost came upon the virgin, and the power of the Highest overshadowed her, it was the Son (Logos) who, laying aside his "form" of God and uniting this divinely wrought (begotten of God) human nature to himself, entered the world through the gateway of a woman's life and became the concentrated expression of the unit work of Godhead and the final and determining factor in his own incarnation," - Phil. 2:7. The resurrection of Christ does not touch His essential and eternal relation to the Father. It is the coming forth of the Son from the grave in the humanity, which, with the Father and the Spirit, He had created for Himself.

"When it is said he is the "first born of every creature (creation)," the qualification is used in the sense not of essence or origin, but in the sense of heirship. - Heb. 1:2. He is the "beginning" of the creation of God." He was the first to rise from the dead. As such He is the "second Adam," the last Adam, the head and beginning of the new race potentially in Him, the new creation of God. ("The primal source of all creatures." - Col. 1:15, - A. S. Worrel.)

"Only God can atone to God. God as God cannot die. He must have a human nature. God must become incarnate. As sons of God we are subject to an dependent on him as that one of whom alone of all the sons of God it can be said, 'Before the mountains were brought forth, or ever thou hadst formed the earth and the world, even from everlasting to everlasting, Thou art God" - Psa. 90:2. - I. M. Haldeman. "And God was the Word.) - John 1:1. "God was manifest in the flesh." - 1 Tim. 3:16.

"The final goal of Greek philosophy was only reached when the great thinkers of the early christian church, who had been trained in the schools of Alexandria and Athens, used its modes of thought in their analysis of the christian idea of God. The result was the evolution of the doctrine of the Trinity." Ency. Britt.

Pastor J. T. Boddy has written the following convictions, which would seem to be very applicable at this time: "All must concede that it is impossible for the finite to comprehend or define the Infinite, and that whatever measure of knowledge of God and the great mystery of godliness procurable in this life, it must reach us by revelation through the Word, and not through reason. We have become too metaphysical. Our salvation does not depend on our correct conceptions of the Godhead, but upon our personal relation to Him through Jesus Christ.

"Many very incompetent persons mentally and spiritually, have irreverently "rushed in where angels fear to tread," and have undertaken to analyze, define and even dissect God, and then presumptuously held up before Him their human analysis, in sacrilegious attitude. This is largely due to a lack of true veneration and reverence for divine and sacred things. And this is frequently done by so over-emphasizing a truth that we warp it out of its true relation to the other truths, and thereby weaken the whole."

From Binney's Compend we gather the following instructive Bible study on the subject: "Jesus Christ is verily and truly man. Jesus Christ is the very unoriginated God. - John 1:1; 20:28, Acts 20:28, Rom. 9:5 (the Spanish translation reads, "Who is God over all things, blessed forever"), Col. 2:9, Phil. 2:6, 1 Tim. 3:16, Titus 2:10, Heb. 1:8, 1 John 5:20.

"His eternity is proven by the following Scriptures: Isa. 9:6, Micah 5:2, John 1:1; John 8:58, Col. 1:17, Heb. 7:3; 13:8; Rev. 1:8. His divine titles are given, a few of which are Alpha and Omega. - Rev. 1:8; 21:6; 22:13. Emmanuel, - Matt. 1:23. First and last, - Rev. 1:17. Everlasting Father, Isa. 9:6. Mighty God, Isa. 9:6. King of kings and Lord of lords, - 1 Tim. 6:15. Lord of Glory, - 1 Cor. 2:8. Prince of Life, Acts 3:15. And many other titles and passages. He is proven Omnipresent, Omniscient, and Omnipotent, by many Scriptures

"Substantial divinity and real humanity are combined in the person of Jesus Christ. As man he weeps over the grave of Lazarus. As God, He raises him from the dead. As man he himself suffers and dies. But as God He is able to raise His own body from the dead. - John 10:18. As those two natures are united in him, he has of course a double mode of speaking of himself.

"Jesus manifestly claims supreme divinity where he says to Philip, "he that hath seen me hath seen the Father" - John 14:9. Jesus was the human personation of the invisible God. Philip sees the Father only as he sees him in the Son. - John 1:18. In his mediatorial office, being sent, he was inferior to the Father who sent him. - John 14:28. He refers not to his nature but to his office, - "the Father is greater than I." In view of Christ's many claims to be God, he is either God, or not a good man. They who begin by denying Christ's supreme Deity logically end by assailing his moral integrity. - Mark 10:18. In Mark 13:32, the ignorance does not disprove his Divinity: It may have been a part of his humiliation in His mediatorial office. The union of two whole and perfect natures, divinity and humanity, qualify Jesus Christ to be the mediator. That is, perfectly to represent God to sinful man, and fallen man to God, and to provide, through his shed blood, and the agency of-the Holy Spirit, for a reconciliation between them. - 1 Tim. 2:5, - Notes from Binney's Compend.

Iraneaus, a disciple of Polycarp, who was a disciple of St. John, wrote: "God was to become man, and in Christ he became man. Christ must be God; for if not, the devil would have had a natural claim on him, and he would have been no more exempt from death than the other children of Adam; he must be man if his blood were indeed to redeem us. In the God-man God has drawn man up to himself. The Logos is the voice of God, with which the Father speaks in the revelation to mankind." Jesus was a "cross" between God and man. God "crossed" himself with humanity. "God was manifest in the flesh." - 1 Tim. 3:16.

The Editor of the Sunday School Times writes: "John introduces Christ to us as the Word. The Greek word logos, translated word,' had two meanings. It signified the intelligence or the reason. Our word logic is derived from it in this sense. It also signified speech. Both these meanings are included when John calls Christ the Word. He is the inward Word of God, because He exists from all eternity in the bosom of the Father, as much one with Him as reason is one with the reasoning mind. Nothing is so close to man as his own thought. So nothing is so close to God as His own, eternal Word. It is within Him, it is one with Him, and it is divine, like Him. Christ is also God's outward Word. He expresses and explains and reveals to the world what God is."

Alexander Cruden writes in his "Concordance of the Scriptures": The eternal Son of God in his divine nature is equal with the Father; but in his human nature subordinate and inferior to the Father. Both natures are united in the person of Christ. The Word, the eternal Son of God, is equal and consubstantial with the Father, being the express image of the Father, as our word, are of our thoughts." - Heb. 1:3.

On Isa. 9:6, Cruden says: "His name shall be called Wonderful, the Mighty God, that is, He is wonderful, he is the mighty God."

Tertullian wrote, A. D. 200: "There is but one God and no other besides the maker of the world, who produced the universe out of nothing, by his Word sent forth first of all. This by the patriarchs, was always heard in the prophets (1 Peter 1:10-12), at last was sent down, from the Spirit and power of God the Father, into the Virgin Mary, was made flesh in her womb, and born of her, lived (appeared) as Jesus Christ, etc."

Origen, wrote, A. D., 230: "Emptying himself he (Jesus Christ) became man incarnate, while he was yet God and though made man, remained God as he was before." the true Son of the true Father.'

Gregorious wrote, A. D. 270: "One Lord (Jesus Christ), the mighty Word, the wisdom which comprehends the constitution of all things, and the power which produces all creation, the true Son of the true Father."

Fourth Ecumenical Council, A. D. 451: Established Creed of Chalcedon - Christological. The Incarnation: "The God-man is not a mere indwelling of God in man, but an actual and abiding union of the two in one personal life. The Logos assumed, not a human person (else we would have two persons a divine and a human), but human nature which is common to us all; and hence he redeemed, not a particular man but all men as partakers of the same natur

"Christ is not a double being with two persons. He is person, both divine and human. The divine will ever remain divine, and the human ever human, and yet the two have continually one common life. It is a permanent state, resulting from the incarnation. The two natures constitute but one personal life and yet remain distinct

"The self-consciousness of Christ is never divided. The divine nature is the seat of self consciousness and pervades and animates the human. The one divine human person of Christ wrought miracles by virtue of his divine nature, and suffered through his human nature. "The superhuman effect and infinite merit must be ascribed to his divinity. His humanity alone made him capable of temptation, suffering, and death. Christ's human nature had no independent personality of its own besides the divine. The divine nature is the root and basis of his personality.

"His human personality was completed and perfected by being so incorporated with the pre-existent Logos personality as to find in it alone its full self consciousness, and to be permeated and controlled by it in every stage of its development. The human nature of Christ did not exist at all before the act of the incarnation. The Son of God was crucified and buried, yet he suffered not in his Godhead, but in weakness of human nature." So Jesus took on him humanity, not a single human individuality. The human was blended, "crossed,' with the divine. Jesus was "perfect God and perfect man." As such he was capable of the fulness of Divine felicity and blessedness, and yet of the sum total of human wretchedness and suffering. He was "made sin for us, who knew no sin." - 2 Cor. 5:21.

Weymouth Translation, N. T., foot-note on Matt. 1:21: "The full significance of the name "Jesus" is seen in the original "Yeho-shua," which means "Jehovah the Savior," and not merely Savior."

Scofield Reference Bible, foot notes " Matt. 1:21 "Jesus, Greek form of Hebrew Je-hoshua, meaning Savior. Josh. 1:1: Joshua - Je-hoshua

"The central theme of the Bible is Christ. It is this manifestation of Jesus Christ, his person as "God manifest in the flesh," has sacrificial death and his resurrection, which constitute the Gospel. Unto this all preceding Scripture leads, from this all following Scripture proceeds. Man was made in the image and likeness of God. This image is found, chiefly in man's tri-unity, and in his moral nature. Jehovah is distinctly the redemption name of Deity. Jehovah is the self-existent One who reveals Himself.

"Christ is seen in his person as Son of God, and very God. Those Scriptures which attribute to God bodily parts are metaphorical. Jesus was the Mighty God. Jesus the Logos was the expression or utterance of the Person and thought of Deity in his incarnation. Christ applied to himself the Jehovistic "I Am." He claimed to be the Adonai (Lord) of the O. T. Eternal life is the life of God revealed in Jesus Christ, who is God.

"The Memorial Name of God: "The primary meaning of the name Jehovah (English - Lord) is "the self-existent One." Literally (as in Ex. 3:14) He that is who He is, therefore the eternal I Am. But Havah, from whence Jehovah, or Yahwe, is formed, signifies also "to become," that is to become known, thus, pointing to a continuous and increasing self-revelation. Combining these meanings of Havah we arrive at the meaning of the name Jehovah. He is "the self-existent One who reveals Himself. Jehovah Elohim clearly indicates a special relation of Deity, in His Jehovah character, to man, and all Scripture emphasizes this Jehovah is distinctly the redemption name of Deity. When sin entered and redemption became necessary, it was Jehovah Elohim who sought the erring ones, and clothed them with coats of skins." The first distinct revelation of Himself by His name Jehovah was in connection with the redemption of the covenant people out of Egypt. Christ Himself affirmed his deity. He applied to Himself the Jehovistic "I Am."

"The Greek term Logos (Word) means a thought or concept, and the expression or utterance of that thought. Christ is from eternity, but especially in his incarnation, the utterance or expression of the Person and thought of Deity. The "mystery of God" is Christ, as incarnating the fulness of the Godhead. The life is called "eternal" because it was from the eternity which is past unto the eternity which is to come - it is the life of God revealed in Jesus Christ, who is God

1 Cor. 15:24, 15:28; "The Son will deliver up the kingdom to "God, even the Father" that "God" (i. e., the triune God, Father, Son and Holy Spirit), "my be all in all." The eternal throne is that "of God, and of the' Lamb." - Rev. 22:1." - Scofield Ref. Bible

"The Angel of the Covenant, Jesus Christ, appeared many times in the Old Dispensation, and received worship, as God. "Behold, I send an angel (messenger) before thee ... provoke him not . . . . for My Name is in him." - Ex. 3:20-22. Israel worshipped this angel all the way to the promised land." - Eusebia. This was evidently the Angel of the covenant, Jesus Christ; according to Adam Clarke and others.

The Syriac Version gives the following curious rendering of John 1:18, "No man hath ever seen God; the only begotten God, he who is in the bosom of the Father, he hath declared him." Even the title of this ancient and valuable translation reads as follows: "The New Testament; or, the Book of the Holy Gospel of our Lord and our God, Jesus the Messiah."

Dr. Philip Schaff writes, on John 20:28: "This is the strongest Apostolic confession of faith in the Lordship and divinity of Christ. "Thomas answered and said unto him (Jesus), "My Lord and my God." Thomas could not have uttered a profanity unrebuked by the Lord. He was an honest inquirer for the truth, not an unbeliever. He embraced with, joy the proof.

"It was by a true, divine instinct that the early theologians made Christ Himself, in his divine human personality, the center of their creeds." - Schaff.

Ignatius said: "Be ye deaf, therefore, when any man speaketh to you apart from Jesus Christ." The doctrine of one God undermines the heathen systems of worship at one stroke. When the heathen ask the name of the christians' God the missionaries invariably and rightly tell them Jesus. 1 John 5:20, "This is the true God, and eternal life." - (Jesus.) "Little children, keep yourselves from idols (false ideas of God)." - 20th Century Trans. - 1 John 5:21

Wm. Smith. LL. D., in his Bible Diet., writes as follows: "Throughout the Hebrew Scriptures two chief names are used for the one true divine being - Elohim, commonly translated God in our Version, and Jehovah, translated Lord. Jehovah denotes specifically the one true God, whose people the Jews were, and who made them the guardians of His truth. The name is never applied to a false god, nor to any other being, except One, the Angel Jehovah, who is thereby marked as one with God, and who appears again in the New Covenant as "God manifest in the flesh."

"The Jews' abstained from pronouncing this name, for fear of its irreverent use. "The Name", (Shema), is substituted by the Rabbis for the unutterable word. They also call it "the name of four letters" (JHVH), "the great and terrible name," "the peculiar name," "the separate name." In reading the Scriptures they substituted for it Adonai (Lord). The substitution of the word is most unhappy. The mind has constantly to guard against a confusion with its lower uses. The key to the meaning of the name is unquestionably given in God's revelation of Himself to Moses by the phrase, "I am that I am," in connection with the statement that He was now first revealed by His name Jehovah. - Ex. 3:14; Ex. 6:3, ((John 8:58)). Jehovah expresses the essential, eternal, unchangeable Being of Jehovah. It is also a practical revelation of God, in His essential, unchangeable relation to His chosen people, the basis of His covenant. He was about, for the first time, fully to reveal that aspect of His character which the name implied - Jehovah." The name Jehovah had been known from the beginning. - Gen 2

Rev. Leon Tucker, prominent Baptist preacher and writer, in his book "Is Jesus Christ Creature or Creator?" writes the following: "Apart from the Scriptures we can know nothing of Jesus Christ. Apart from Jesus Christ we can know nothing of the Scriptures. The Word of God and the Son of God are eternal and inseparable, therefore to the child of God the Scriptures are imperative. The battle continues with ever increasing hate and hostility. The personal attributes of the Son of God are not only little understood, but much misunderstood. The means of the revelation of God is Christ. He is not only the conveyor of that revelation, but is the revelation itself.

"Scripture declares He was in the world from all time, existed before all time, and will be when time is no more. The Eternal Christ is the theme of the Scriptures. It takes a whole Bible to give us a whole Christ. Christ is from Eternity to Eternity in His character. Henry Ward Beecher in writing the Life of Christ said, "How can I finish the Life of Christ? a life which never began, and will never end." "But thou, Bethlehem-Ephratah ... out of thee shall one come forth unto me, that is to be ruler in Israel; whose goings forth are from of old, from everlasting (the days of eternity)." - Micah 5:2

"The Son was in the "bosom of the Father" because never unborn. Jesus Christ came from the "bosom of the Father." He was God manifest in the flesh, but nevertheless God of all flesh, and before all flesh. He was not manifestation of God in the flesh, but was. "God manifest in the flesh." He was before all things. - Col. 1:17. Isaiah refers to Him as "Father of Eternity." - Isa. 9:6. - Heb. Eternal life is "in the Son." - 1 John 5:11, John 17:3. Natural life, spiritual life, and eternal life all come front Him. All the attributes of God are His and He is God.

"He pre-existed as God. - John 1:1. He was predicated as God - Isa. 9:6. He professed to be

God. - John 5:18. He was proclaimed God. - 1 Tim. 3:16. He was promoted as God. - Heb. 1:8, 9. He was petitioned as God. - 1 Cor. 1:2. His perfections are God's. - John 8:53[sic], John 8.58[sic], 10:15, 28; John 20:28. Matt. 18:20, Heb. 7:26. He created. - Col. 1:15, 17. He is "Providence," - Heb. 1:3.

"Jesus Christ the same yesterday, today, and forever." - Heb. 13:8. Human reason has always failed at the Christ. But the fact remains. Divine revelation can never sink to human reason, and human reason can never rise to divine revelation. The Bible says He is a Creator. - Col 1:15-20. The Bible says He is God. He is no less than the Creator of all things, whether they be atoms or angels, persons or planets. The Seraphim at the presence of His glory, covered their faces. - Isa. 6:1-8. John 12:39-41.

"In the beginning God," (Gen 1:1), and Christ is the beginning. He is before all time. He is the Alpha of all things. There was some one before there was anything. He was the One. Angels both faithful and fallen know Him if men do not. He is Lord of All. No, Jesus Christ is not a creature, He is the Creator. Whether in Creation or Redemption, Jesus Christ is the Absolute and all perfect expression of God. He is all of God and God is all of Christ. Let us speak out in these days of doubt and declension. The Christology of the Book is better than the philosophy of all books. Christ is "All and in all." - Leon Tucker

John Bunyan: "His (Jesus') attributes, though apart laid down in the Word of God, that we, being weak, might the better conceive of his eternal power and Godhead; yet in him they are without division, one glorious and eternal being. The Godhead is but one, yet in the Godhead there are three. These three are called the Father, the Son, and the Holy Spirit; each of which is really, naturally and eternally God; yet there is but one God. To each the Scripture applieth, and that truly, the whole nature of Dei

"Adam heard the voice of the Lord God walking in the midst of the garden; which voice John will have to be one of the three, calling that which Moses here saith is the voice, the Word of God: "In the beginning was the Word," the voice which Adam heard walking in the midst of the garden. This "Word was with God," - "Word was God." - John 1:1,2.

"Now the godly in former ages have called these three, in the Godhead, Persons or Subsistences; the which though I condemn not yet choose rather to abide by Scripture phrase. Thou must take heed when thou readest that there is in the Godhead, Father, Son, and Holy Spirit, that thou do not imagine about them, according to thine own carnal and foolish fancy, and foolishly imagine about it. You find not one of the prophets propounding an argument to prove it; but asserting it, they let it lie, for faith to take it up and embrace it. The Godhead then, though it can admit of a Trinity, yet it admitteth not of inferiority in that Trinity; if otherwise then there must be less or more, and so either plurality of gods, or something that is not God."

The infidel Renan "declared: ", Thou Man of Galilee, Thou hast conquered; and henceforth no man shall be able to distinguish between thee and God. Banner of our contradictions! Thou wilt be the sign around which there will be fought the fiercest battles." And it is so.

Napoleon, on the Island of St. Helena, in exile, said: "Alexander, Caesar, Charlemange and I have founded great empires; but upon what did these creations depend? Upon force. Jesus has founded his empire upon love, and to this very day millions would die for him. No one else is like Him. Jesus Christ was more than a man. I have inspired multitudes with such devotion that they would have died for me. But to do this it was necessary that I should be visibly present, with the electric influence of my looks, of my words, of my voice. Christ alone has succeeded in so raising the mind of man toward the unseen that it becomes insensible to the barriers of time and space. Across a chasm of 1800 years Jesus Christ makes a demand which is, above all others, difficult to satisfy. He demands it unconditionally, and forthwith his demand is granted. Time, the great destroyer, is powerless to extinguish the sacred flame. This it is which strikes me most."

Some one has written of Napoleon: "Moved alternately by admiration, jealousy, and remorse at Jesus Christ, Napoleon unhesitatingly and in all sincerity denominated him "the man-God." He marveled at the power of the symbol of the Cross to change mens' lives. The thing that aroused his jealousy, admiration and remorse, was the fact that while he had led the world's greatest armies to the slaughter and miserably failed either to retain a kingdom or the adherence of his followers, Jesus Christ had given his own life and secured an eternal kingdom, and the lasting admiration and fidelity of a world of true believers. Napoleon began by desiring to be a god. He ended by being hated and execrated by all."

Editor E. N. Bell wrote as follows on Isa. 9:6: "Jesus was and is the Everlasting Father in the sense that he is the father of eternity, but not the Father of our Lord Jesus Christ. The idea is that Jesus existed before all time, though in the flesh he appeared in time; also that he originated or created all things. Isa. 9:6 does not discuss or refer to the Father in the N. T. sense. He is the father also of the "new creation," even as the "first Adam" was of the old."

Wm. H.' Bennett, an English writer says: "The Everlasting Father," Isa. 9:6, "The Father of the Everlasting Age, the One from whom spring the glory and blessedness of God's new creation."

Adam Clarke, speaking of the name for Jesus in the O. T., writes: "This is the famous tetragrammaton, or name of four letters, which we write Jehovah. The letters are JHVH. The Jews never pronounce it; and the true pronunciation is utterly unknown. This name the Jews never attempt to pronounce. When they meet with it in the Bible they read Adonai for it. To a man they all declare that no man can pronounce it; and that the true pronunciation has been lost; and that God alone knows its true interpretation and pronunciation." It is evidently a mouthful for the Jews. It is "Jesus

Dr. Chas. H. Spurgeon, the great London preacher, wrote on 1 Timothy 3:16: "Was it a man that was manifest in the flesh? Assuredly not, for every man is manifest in the flesh. This could not be called a mystery. Was it an angel? What angel was ever manifest in the flesh? And if it were would it be a mystery for him to be seen of angels? Could it have been the devil? If so, be has been: "received up into glory," which, let us hope is not the case. Now, if it was neither of these three that was "manifest in the flesh," then it must have been God."

Declaration of Evangelical Association of the World: "Christ is supreme in God's revelation to Man. Christ declared of himself: "He that seeth me seeth the Father also." He was the brightness of the Father's glory, and the express image of his person. Christ revealed the Fatherhood of God, of God, as well as the Saviorhood of man. There is no higher revelation of God than we have in Jesus Christ. "God was in Christ reconciling the world unto himself," and the historical and experimental fact is a unique, and an unmatched revelation of God in the creation and redemption of man, the correct interpretation of God's eternal purpose with man. Christ is the supreme revealer of God in human redemption.

Wyckliffe: "Our faith will not fail for it is founded on Jesus alone, our Master and our God. The mediator must needs be a man; but every man, being indebted to God for everything that he is able to do this man must needs have infinite merit, and be at the same time God."

Jacob Boehme, A. D. 1624. "The way to oneness is to sink into the knowledge of the great and holy name of God, Jehovah or Jesus, as the living Word, that gives life to all things. In the only beloved Son, God is revealed."

Hannah Whitall Smith: "The God who created us is the God who saves us. Not another God, for there is none beside Him, but the very God, our Creator himself. Some are apt to think of our Creator and our Savior as two Gods, with interests which are not identical. But we are told as plainly as words can tell it, that the Creator is also the Savior, and there is none beside."

Chas. G. Finney, the Great Revivalist: "Only the Holy Ghost can reveal Christ as God so that the believing soul will be fast established in this truth and the fact become a sanctifying power in the heart."

Pastor Paul, of Berlin, in a Book recently written, declares: "The Antichrist is about to set himself up as a man-God, and in keeping with this assumption his chief attack will be to overthrow the fact that Jesus Christ is God." Antichrist will set himself forth in the temple of God as God. "He that opposeth and exalteth himself against all that is called God, so that he sitteth in the temple of God, setting himself forth as God." - 2 Thessalonians 2:4. Then let us set Jesus Christ forth in our temple as the true God. Anti-christ is "against Christ." "This is the true God, and eternal life," - Jesus, - 1 John 5:20. "Little children, keep yourselves from idols (false ideas of God)." - 1 John 5:21, - 20th Century Trans. Antichrist is subtly and surely paving the way for the complete denial of the Deity of Christ. It will become harder and more unpopular continually to preach this truth. God grant that our sympathies may be found on the right side, that we may not be found finally aiding the Antichrist. Any tendency or spirit to deny the full claims of Jesus Christ is necessarily antichrist, and in line with the Apostasy. The spirit of Antichrist rises up against and opposes the revelation of Jesus Christ, as God. It is a persecuting spirit, the "Mother Harlot" spirit. Just' in the measure that men reject and oppose this full revelation of Christ they still possess the spirit of Antichrist, inherited through the "fall," enmity with God.

Testimony of Suzuki Yasukei, a Japanese convert in Japan: "I am a man of 78 years of age and getting very old. I have been a member of Japanese old Buddhist temple for over 60 years, and I have learned many Korans, and I can pray like priests for the dead people and instruct others how they can go to a place where people live on water lily flowers all the time. That is what we call "Gokuraku," a place of easy retirement. I thought it was the true way and no other way to go to that fine place, so I worshipped Buddha every morning, beating drum and burning incense, repeating the same each year without knowing peace in my heart. I thought, I can go to that place in this way. But this year in May I heard that a Christian tent meeting was going on at Kitagata Yochien waki, where people were finding real joy and peace through Yaso (Jesus Christ). I went to the tent, and found the true God and Savior. Although I wasted my whole life, thank God he has saved me even now before I die. He has become my personal Redeemer.

"A few days ago I saw a wonderful dream or vision. It was so real to me I will tell you all about it. I awakened early: and was meditating on God when I saw something with my eyes. As I looked up I saw a beautiful country and many people shouting hallelujah, as I heard in the mission, and I wanted to go there so much. Then at this time two priests -came in to talk to me from the sidewalk and asked me. "Do you forsake us? Where are you going now? Come on with us to the temple." But I said to them, You are dirty, wicked deceitful priests. You misled me, you fooled me, you cheated me; get out of my way. I hollered out like, that. Again Yaso (Jesus) appeared in a cloud, and took me on that same cloud to that beautiful, country which I had seen a few moments before. Oh, it was so beautiful! I never saw such a beautiful place since I was born. Jesus himself said to me, "You were honest, so I will give you a key to the treasure house of this country." At this time I really found out the true God and Savior, Jesus Christ. I heard many people say, Kami (God), Yaso (Jesus), Miseire (Holy Spirit); I thought they were all different gods. But God is united with Yaso (Jesus) on the throne of God." - From "The Toyo No Koe," Japan. This old Japanese saint's photo was printed with the article.

Sadhu Sundar Singh: "Sadhu Sundar Singh is known as the St. Paul of India. His life and experience have been apparently parallel to those of Apostolic days. He has visited the Orient, the Isle of Ceylon, European countries and, also the U. S. In a book written by a well known writer, the following is what Sundar Singh has to say on the subject of the Trinity: "At one time I was a good deal perplexed about the doctrine of the Trinity. I had thought of three separate persons, sitting as it were on three thrones, but it was all made plain to me in a vision. I entered into an ecstasy into the third heaven. I was told, it was the same to which St. Paul was caught up. And there I saw Christ in a glorious body sitting on a throne. Whenever I go there it is the same. Christ is always in the center, a figure ineffable and indescribable, His face shining like the Sun, but in no way dazzling, and so sweet that without any difficulty I can gaze at it - always smiling a glorious, loving smile.

"The first time I entered heaven I looked around and I asked; "But where is God?" And they told me, "God is not to be seen here any more than on earth, for God is Infinite. But there is Christ, He is God. He is the image of the invisible God, and it is only in Him that we can see God, in Heaven as on earth." And streaming out from Christ I saw, as it were, waves shining and peace giving, and going through and among the saints and angels, and everywhere bringing refreshment, just as in hot weather water refreshes trees; and this I understood to be the Holy Spirit."

Some one has beautifully and truly written the following: "The central theme of the Word of God is Jesus Christ. In Genesis He is the Creator, in Exodus He is the Passover Lamb, in Leviticus He is the Offering, in Numbers He is represented in type, in Deuteronomy He fills the reviews, in Joshua He is the Captain of the Lord's Host, in Judges He is the Righteous Judge, in Ruth He is the Husband, in Samuel He is the Prophet of the prophets, in Kings and Chronicles He is the King of kings and Lord of lords, in Ezra He is the Restorer of His people, in Nehemiah He is the Protector of His people, in Esther He is the Preserver of His people, in Job He is the Redeemer that liveth, in Psalms He is the Shepherd King-Messiah, in Proverbs He is the Wise Man, in Ecclesiastes He is the only One under the sun in whom there is no vanity, in Songs of Solomon He is the Bridegroom-Lover. The major and minor or the pre-exilic, exilic, and post-exilic prophets especially portray in minute and comprehensive detail the exact events that cluster around the two advents of Christ. In Matthew He is the King-Messiah, in Mark He is the Servant-Messiah, in Luke He, is the Man-Messiah, and in John He is the God-Messiah. The historic, epistolary and apocalyptic letters all reveal the one personage. - Jesus Christ."

CHAPTER III

J. Merle D'Aubigne, author of "History of the Reformation," wrote in the middle of the 19th century: "What is Jesus Christ if He be not God in history? Is not this great truth, that God has appeared in human nature, in reality the keystone of the arch? History records a birth of God, and yet God has no part in history. Jesus Christ is the true God of man's history. God appeared among men, and as man, to save that which was lost. In Jesus of Nazareth dwelt all the fulness of the Godhead bodily."

Martin Luther declared: "Christ is the one, sole, and true God (1 John 5:20). When you have Him for your God, you have no other gods." He also declared, "Thy repentance and thy works may deceive thee, but Christ, thy God, wilt not deceive thee." To Pope Leo, Luther wrote, "Christ who is God and man. Christ who has never sinned, and whose holiness is immaculate. Christ the Almighty and Everlasting."

Melancthon, Luther's co-laborer, "quoted often Homer, Plato, Cicero, Pliny and others, for he was a great scholar, but Christ ever remained his Master and his God." - D'Aubigne.

Zwingle declared: "Christ, who is very God, and very man. Since it was the eternal God who died for us, his passion is therefore an eternal sacrifice. - Acts 20:28. Proceeding from the Father, he (Christ) is God, and consequently present in every place. According to his human nature, he was absent from heaven while be was upon the earth, and quitted the earth when he ascended into heaven; but, according to his divine nature, he remained in heaven when he came down thence (the Logos), and did not abandon the earth, when he returned thither."

Staupitz, the spiritual father of Luther, said: "We cannot understand God outside of Jesus Christ. In Him, the Lord has said, you will find what I am, and what I require. Nowhere else, neither in heaven nor in earth, will you discover it."

Dr. Albert Eby, Wilshire Presby. Church Pastor, writes: "The only perfect man in all history or experience was God Himself, manifest in the flesh. He is also revealed as the indwelling Holy Spirit."

Wm. Conant, in his Magazine, "Salvation," some years ago wrote the following: "It is the grand theological error of separating the Father and the Son, as two in this sacrifice (the atonement), in the suffering of it and the love in it, that has perverted the doctrine to an impossibility for the moral mind, and has been answerable for the defection of millions of souls from the Gospel of Christ. An intelligent Scriptural correction of this error in the theology of the church must be the means of arresting the present already stupendous apostasy."

Wm. H. Bennett, a well known English writer, in his book, "The Person of the Lord Jesus Christ," has written as follows: "The Lord Jesus Christ was when on earth, and is now in heaven, absolutely, both God and man. He is truly God. He is truly man. From His incarnation and birth He was, He is, and He ever will be both God and man.

"In Isa. 6, we read that the prophet saw. One seated upon a throne, high and lifted up, before Whom seraphim covered themselves. That this was the very One who afterwards trod the earth in humiliation, is declared by the Apostle John. - John 12:41, Isa. 7:14; Isa. 9:6. "Jehovah our Righteousness." - Jer. 23:6. "In the beginning was the Word, the Word was with God, and the Word was God." - John 1:1. The beginning of which John speaks is a beginning that is beginningless, not the beginning of creation (Gen. 1:1). The "Word was." Essential being was His. "Before Abraham was I Am." - John 8:58. He is revelation of God. - John 1:18.

"The Lord Jesus is spoken of chiefly as the Son of God, But this expression denotes nothing less than oneness, with the Father, and possession of all the attributes of Godhead." I and the Father are one.". -_ John 10:30, - Greek. "The Jews. answered him "For a good work we stone thee not, but for blasphemy; and because that thou, being a man, makest thyself God." - John 10:33. They had understood that he applied to himself that title by which Jehovah was revealed to Moses - (Ex. 3). "Before Abraham was I am" - John 8:58. The Jews understood his meaning. - John 1:36 (He was the Logos, the Word that "was God." - John 1:1, "equal with God." John 5:18, Phil. 2:6.)

"St. Paul is declaring that in the Son there dwells all the fullness of absolute Godhead, they were no mere rays of Divine glory which gilded Him, lighting up His Person for a season and with a splendor not His own, but He was, and is, absolute and perfect God." The Son of God is the exact and full expression of what God is, which He could not be if He were not Himself God.

"In Rev. 1, Christ is associated with the eternal God as the equal source of grace and peace; in Rev. 5, He is equally with Him who sits on the throne, the object of universal worship; in Rev. 22, He is seen as sharing with God the throne of the new creation. In Rev. 22:13, He describes Himself by the words which in Rev. 1:8 are the utterance of the Lord God. "I am the Alpha and the Omega." While in that same verse, as well as in Rev. 1:17, He declares Himself to be "the First and the Last." This prerogative is three times claimed for the Lord Jehovah, in Isa. 41:4; Isa. 44:6; Isa. 48:12, and in like manner three times in Revelation, 1:17; 2:8; 22:13. It is the expression of absolute Godhead, "I am the First and the Last, and beside Me there is no god" (Isa. 44:6). He is from eternity to eternity, so that there is no room for any other.

"Godhead in all its fulness, and manhood in all its perfectness, are united in the Christ of God. He appeared to Ezekiel by the river Chebar with "the likeness as the appearance of a man" (Ezek. 1:1, 26), as He had previously manifested Himself to Moses in the bush, and to Isaiah in the temple. But when He came into the world to dwell for a season, He took on "flesh." Phil. 2:5-11, - "made himself of no reputation" is what is meant by "emptying himself." He had not and could not empty Himself of His Godhead. He became what He before was not; but He had not ceased to be what He was. He divested Himself of all outward expressions of Divine glory. He abased Himself.

"In all revelations of God it was by the Son that He revealed Himself. - John 1:18. Gen. 1:1:2, - one of these was the Lord. Gen. 16:7; 32:24, Ex. 3:2, Joshua 5:15. These were all appearances of the Angel of Jehovah (Jesus Christ), in a form suitable to the occasion. It is true that Daniel had a glorious vision of "one like unto the Son of Man" (a son of man.' - R. V.), receiving the kingdom from "The Ancient of Days," but he is careful to tell us that it was a dream and visions of his head upon his bed." - Dan. 7:13, 14.

" Heb. 1:2, He is declared to be the Son, but in v. 8, He is addressed as God. Heb. 1:10 (Ps. 102:25), He is addressed as Jehovah. Bishop Beveridge says, "If Jesus were God only, and not man, He could not suffer anything whereby to satisfy Divine justice; if man only and not God, He could not satisfy even though He suffered. If man only, His satisfaction could not be sufficient for God; if God only, it would not be suitable for man. And therefore to be capable of suffering for man, and able to satisfy God, Himself must be both God and man." He was "the Man that is My fellow." - Zech. 13:7. (John 10:30.)

The deeper our sense of the true glory and fulness of our Lord, the deeper will be our confidence in Him, and the truer will be our confidence in Him, and the truer will be our reverence in speaking of Him." - W. H. Bennett.

Dr. A. C. Dixon, speaking of Sir Oliver Lodge said "But I want to know, does this man believe in Jesus Christ as the eternal God, who made the world and the ether; and the atoms, and everything else that was made. And does he bow his knee and worship Him? If he does not, he is on the other side - against God.

"You don't need anybody if you will just take "Jesus only." And what we need is not to consult with spirits, but trust the Holy Spirit of God, looking up into the face of Jesus and worship Him, and love Him, and serve Him, and "Jesus only" will make us triumphant over sin, and sorrow, and death, and hell. Jesus only is what we need." - Christian Alliance Weekly.

Editor Stanley Frodsham: "Every Bible student knows that since no man hath seen God (the Father) at any time, that the Lord Jehovah who manifested Himself to prophet and patriarch so often in olden times, was none other than the only begotten Son, our Lord and Savior Jesus Christ, who is the one, according to John, who has declared or made the Father known (John 1:18).

Pastor Harry Morse writes: "Today I see a Christ that is high over all, with all power in heaven and earth, Matt. 28:18; and with a name that is above every name. - Phil. 2:9. People are trying to strip our Lord of His divinity, and also one is about to come in his own name." - John 5:43. This being will be the Antichrist. - 1 John 2:18."

God calls Himself Israel's Savior, - "For I am the Lord thy God, the Holy One of Israel, thy Savior. - Isa. 43:3. "I, even I, am the Lord; and beside me there is no savior." - Isa. 43:11. "A just God and a savior; there is none beside me." - Isa. 45:21. "For this is good and acceptable in the sight of God our Savior." - I Tim. 2:3. "According to the commandment of God our Savior." - Titus 1:3. "That they may adorn the doctrine of God our Savior." - Titus 2:10. "Looking for the blessed hope and appearing of the glory of our great God and Savior Jesus Christ." - Titus 2:13 R. V. "But when the kindness of God our Savior." - Titus 3:4. "To the only wise God our Savior, be glory and greatness, might and authority, both now, and to all ages." - Jude 25 (Greek).

Shepherd: Compare Isa. 40:10, 11, with John 10:11, I Peter 5:4. Rock: " II Sam. 22:47, Ps. 62:2; 78:35. "They drank of that spiritual Rock that followed them; and that Rock was Christ." - 1 Cor. 10:4. Some think the children of Israel got their water continually from this Rock in the desert. King: "And the Lord shall be king over all the earth; in that day shall the Lord be one, and his name one." - I Cor. 2:8. "Until the appearing of our Lord Jesus Christ; which in its own times he shall show who is the blessed and only Potentate, the King of kings, and Lord of lords." - I Tim. 6:14, 15, R.V. "And he hath on his vesture and on his thigh a name written, King of kings and Lord of lords." - Rev. 19:16. The I AM: " Ex. 3:14 6:3; John 8:58 . The First and Last: Isa. 41:4; 43:10, 44:6; Isa. 48:12, Rev. 1:17; Rev. 22:13."

Pastor D. W Kerr: "There are some things of which the written word of God speaks, which are, and always will be, too deep and high for us to understand. He has not told us how He can be a Father without beginning, nor how He can. Have a Son without beginning; nor how there can be a Holy Ghost without beginning. In other words, the Bible does not tell us how there can be a Father, a Son, and a Holy Ghost, who always was, is now, and ever shall be, Father, Son and Holy Ghost. The Veil is the flesh of Christ. - Heb. 10:20, It in the "Word made flesh." On the one side, God. On the other side man, the God-man."

Justin Martyr, beheaded at Rome, A. D., 167, wrote: That ye might also know God, who came from above and became man among men. And who is again to return, when they who pierced Him shall see and bewail Him."

Clemens Alexandrinus, a friend of Iraneaus (who suffered martyrdom A. D., 202), says: "Believe, O man, in Him who is both man and God; believe, O man, in Him who suffered death, and yet is adored as the living God."

Thomas Chatterton, an English poet, wrote: "A humble form the Godhead wore, the pains of poverty He bore, to gaudy pomp unknown. Tho' in a human walk He trod, still was the Man Almighty God, in glory all His own."

Thomas B. Macauly, English historian, writes: "It was before Deity embodied in human form, walking among men, that the prejudices of the synagogue and the doubts of the academy, the faces of the victors and the swords of thirsty legions were humbled in the dust."

Frances B. Willard, American Temperance reformer, said in her last words: "I am safe with Him. I have always believed in Christ. He is the incarnate God."

Chas. H. Spurgeon wrote: "In heaven, in earth, in hell, all knees bend before Him, and every tongue confesses that He (Christ) is God."

"Be a valiant soldier, routing every sin. Sing His praise, sing His praise. Christ the great Jehovah, will be sure to win. Sing His praise, sing His praise." - I. O. Brown.

"Forbid it, Lord, that I should boast, save in the death of Christ, my God. All the vain things that charm me most, I sacrifice them to His blood." - Isaac Watts.

Dictionary of Apostolic Church, by Jas. Hastings, D. D.: "The revelation of the Son is the revelation of the, Father. - 1 John 1:2. "Neither doth any know the Father, save the Son, and he to whomsoever the Son willeth to reveal him." - Matt. 11:27. The Holy Ghost is in one breath called by St. Paul the "Spirit of God," and "the Spirit of Christ." - Rom. 8:9, Titus 3:4-6, Eph. 4:4. "I am in the Father, and the Father in me." - John 14:10."

People who imagine they could view God's unveiled presence and live do not know God. - Deut. 4:12-16. It is said by those who work among them that both Jews and Moslems believe that christians worship three gods (are idolators). Would it not be better to preach to them "God manifest in the flesh," in the person of Jesus Christ?

"The voice of one that crieth, Prepare ye in the wilderness the way of the Lord, make straight in the desert a highway for our God. O thou that tellest good tidings to Zion; say unto the cities of Judah, Behold your God." - , Isa. 40:3, 9; "The voice of one crying in the wilderness, Make ye ready the way of the Lord. Make His paths straight." - Matt. 3:3.

Ancient Jacobite copies of the N. T. read: "For God himself, in his grace, tasted death for all men." - Heb. 2:9. "To feed the church of God, which He purchased with His own blood." - Acts 20:28.

A certain writer has added the following on the subject of the Godhead: "God's one great being is a spiritual Being, and not angelic nor human, but He is just like Himself, and nothing can be compared with Him - Isa. 4:13, 18, 25. "Seven spirits of God" are the complete spiritual essence or subsistence of that one great Spiritual Being, just like the seven churches make a perfect spiritual body of Christ. These seven spirits of God are attributed to Jesus Christ (Rev. 1:4; 3:1; 4:5). "This proves our Lord to be the very God of the "seven spirits" in his Deity. God has "one face." - Rev. 22:4, 2 Cor. 4:6."

"Christ is Jehovah of Glory." - Ps. 24:7, 10; I Cor. 2:8; , J5: 21. Jehovah our Righteousness. - Jer. 23:5, 6, I Cor. 1:30. Jehovah's Fellow and Equal. - Zech. 13:7, Phil. 2:6. Jehovah a Stone of Stumbling. - Isa. 8:13, 14, I Peter 2:8. Jehovah as the Mighty God. - Ps. 50:1, Isa. 9:6, Rev. 1:8. Jehovah as the true God. - "The Lord is the true God, and an everlasting king (king of eternity)" - Jer. 10:10, I John 5:20. Jehovah as Creator. Isa. 40:28, John 3:3, Col 1:16. Jehovah raises Himself from the dead: John 2:19-2; 10:13. Jehovah is Eternal: Isa. 9:6, Micah 5:2, John 1:1, Col 1:17. Jehovah as Husband: Isa: 54:5; 62:5, Eph. 5:25-32, Rev.21:2, 9.

Jesus Christ is the Jehovah-God of the O. T. Scholars have agreed in giving to the Son of

God, Jesus Christ, our Lord the following names, titles, and character: "God. - John 1:1, Matt. 1:23, Isa. 40:3. God whose throne is forever and ever. - Heb. 1:8. The Mighty God. - Isa. 9:6. The Everlasting God. - Isa. 40:28. The true God. - 1 John 5:20. My Lord and God. - John 20:28: God my Savior. - Luke 1:47. God over all. - Rom. 9:5. The God of the whole earth. - Isa; 54:5. God manifest in the flesh. - I Tim. 3:16. Our God and Savior. - II Peter 1:1. Our great God and Savior Jesus Christ. Titus 2:13, R. V.

"Where Jesus is called Jehovah: " Isa. 4:3, 10; 6:3, John 12:41, Zech. 14:5, Hosea 12:4, 5, Gen. 32:24, Ps. 24:8, Jer. 23:6. Other Scriptures applied to Christ: Rev. 1:8, Col 1:16, Heb. 1:3, etc. All these Scriptures have been applied to Jesus Christ by the best scholars and translators we have in the land, outside the Pentecostal Movement.

Another writer pens the following: Christ is God. To deny that Christ is God robs him of all his glory. He is both God and man. It is this veil, or mystery, that has hidden Jehovah from His people, the Jews. - John 1:11, II Cor. 3:14-18. God is veiled in Jesus Christ. "Hear, O Israel: the Lord our God is one Lord." - Deut. 6:4. The personal, visible form of God was Jesus Christ, and today the Christ with us and in us is "that Spirit" (the Holy Spirit) - II Cor. 3:17. "And it shall be said in that day Lo, this is our God; we have waited for him and he will save us, this is the Lord (Jehovah); we have waited for him; we will be glad and rejoice in his salvation." - Isa. 25:6-9.

The Jews declared that they knew God the Father. But Jesus alone can reveal the Father. The Mohammedans claim to know God the Father. But they look upon Jesus' sacrificial death with unspeakable hatred. Jesus Christ is the Mighty God. "He that overcometh shall inherit all things; and I will be his God, and he shall be my son." - Rev. 21:7, Isa. 9:6. It is the "veil of flesh" assumed by the Mighty God that causes men to stumble. - II Cor. 5:16.

A Missionary in India, M. F. Clemenger, recently wrote a brother in Orebro, Sweden: "One comes in touch with individuals who tell us that they believe on Jesus and know that they are saved. Others tell us that they believe that Jesus is the true and living God. Some tell us that they do not know who the living God is; he may be Allah, or Jesus, or some one else. We tell them, "Jesus is the true and living God. He alone has given his life for you." One asked, "If I accept Jesus, am I not to take the name of any other gods?" We told him, "Jesus is the only true God, and he will not give his glory to another." Some say, "The Mohammedans say that Allah is God, you say that Jesus Christ is God, and we say others. How are we to know who is God?" (Did not the missionary do right in telling them that Jesus Christ was God?)

Still another writer adds: "In Ex. 3:13, 14, we read that Moses asked God His name, and God, speaking from the burning bush answered, "I AM THAT I AM. Thus shalt thou say unto the Children of Israel, I AM hath sent me unto you." Our Lord Jesus Christ is the I AM. - John 8:58. No wonder Jews wanted to stone him. They understood him to claim that name for himself. They did not realize that the same I AM who spoke to Moses out of the burning bush, and descended before Moses in the cloud (Ex. 34:5), proclaiming his name, was standing in their midst in the form of a man. There was a terrible splendor about that name that inspired awe and fear. The Jews in times past, as the orthodox Jews do still, reverence that name so much that they do not dare to pronounce it, but substitute in its place "Adonai." Moses admonished the Children of Israel to fear this glorious and fearful name. - Deut. 28:58, Ex. 23:21.

" John 4:26, - "I am, who am speaking unto thee." John 6:20, - "I am; fear not." John 8:28, - "then shall ye know that I am." John 18:5, - "Jesus says to them, I am." John 8:28 John 8:24, 28, - "If ye believe not that I am, ye will die in your sins." "Then ye shall know that I am." These are the literal Greek renderings of the above passages. "I am, the bread of life." "I am, the light of the world." I am, the door." I am, the good shepherd." I am, he resurrection and the life." "I am, the Alpha and the Omega, which is, and which was, and which is to come." "I am, the bright and morning star." - John 6:35, John 9:5; 10:7, 11, John 15:1, Rev. 1:8; Rev. 22:16, In fact, He is everything we need. - Col. 2:9, 10.

Pentecostal Herald: As God made the "first Adam" the father of all living, He made Christ the "second Adam," to all who come to him for eternal life. The first Adam's children all die. But the second Adams children are children of an Eternal Father. Christ is an "Everlasting Father" - Isa. 9:6.

Dr. Joseph G. Kennedy, in "Pentecostal Herald": "Did not Jesus Christ do for man in the New Dispensation what Jehovah did for them in the Old? We cannot escape the conclusion that Jehovah and Jesus Christ are one and the same person. The disciples in their writings ascribed the Jehovah attributes to Jesus Christ.

"Eternal Existence: Gen. 21:33, Rev. 1:18. Creation: Gen. 2:4, John 1:1-3. Omniscience: Ps. 139:1-4, John 2:24, 25. Unchangeableness: Mal. 3:6, Rev. 1:18. Universal Triumph: Ps. 92:9, I Cor. 15:25. Universal Dominion: Zech. 14:9, Rev. 1:18. Universal Supremacy: Ps. 89:6-9, Phil. 2:9. Universal Worship: Ps. 22:27, Phil. 2:10.

"Savior: Isa. 43:11, Luke 19:10. Life: Deut. 30:20, John 1:4. Light: Ps. 27:1; John 9:5. Truth:

Ps 31:5; John 14:6. Forgiver of Sins: Ps. 103:2, 3, Luke 7:47-50, Matt. 9:2-6: Lord of Sabbath: Ex. 20:10, Matt. 12:8. Judge of World: Ps. 98:9, John 5:22, Matt. 16:27. Received Worship: Ps. 99:5, John 9:38, Matt. 28:9, 17, Rev. 5:6-14.

"When Jehovah was revealing the particulars concerning the Messiah which was to come, He must of necessity speak of Him in the third person, though it was Himself that was to be incarnated into human nature, for this indeed was to be a new creation as a God-man, mediator, and sacrifice for sin. Men were saved in O. T. times, as in our day, by faith in God through the Mediator between God and man, knowing little or nothing perhaps of the real meaning of the atonement, yet trusting in the Mediator." - Pentecostal Heral

Missionary R. E. Bass, writes from China: "It would be no mystery if we knew there were simply three separate persons operating in unity and with one thought (in the Godhead). Jesus Christ is the image of "the invisible God." - Col. 1 ;15 I Tim. 1:17; We need to believe and honor Jesus Christ today for what He really is, "the Mighty God," "the true God," "the only wise God." "The Lord, the God of the spirits of the prophets, sent his angel" - Rev. 22:6 I Peter 1:11. "I, Jesus, have sent mine angel." - Rev,.22:16. "To sum up all things in Christ." - Eph. 1:10, R. V. "In Him dwelleth all the fulness of the Godhead bodily." - Col. 2:9. We are to look for the true God and the Father nowhere else but in Jesus Christ. So after all it was God (manifest in the flesh) who laid down His life for us. "Which things angels desire to look into." - I Peter 1:12. (A mystery they cannot understand. The incarnation of Deity.)

Elder D. Vervalin, in Pentecostal Herald: There is but one Holy Spirit; not one Holy Spirit in the Father, another Holy Spirit in the Holy Spirit, and another Holy Spirit in the Son. There is one body and one Spirit. - Eph. 4:4. In Rom. 8:9, the Spirit of God that dwells in us is called the Spirit of Christ.

"There is one God in his trinity. God is a name for Him in his trinity. Father is the name for God as to His essential character: the One who is always unseen and who causes all action and plans all things.

"The Holy Spirit is the name for God as the worker, or doer; the one who acts and performs. There is not a verb in the Bible referring to God's action, but is asserting such action as the Holy Spirit action.

"The special name given to the Holy Spirit to designate the action of giving birth is the "Spirit of Christ." To those who have been born again and have the Spirit of Christ, God gives this same Holy Spirit to personally operate man by filling man's spirit and body with the Holy Spirit, direct personal action of man, for purpose of service, first and primarily to God in worship, and secondarily the service toward men.

Jesus never said He would send us another Spirit, but another Advocate. John 14:16 and I John 2:1.

"The Son is the name of God when He manifests Himself to any of His creatures, taking a form that will enable His creatures to comprehend him. Everything made and brought to sight is by the Son. "All things were made by Him." - John 1:3, Col. 1:16-17, Heb. 1:2, etc.

"Man himself is made in the image of God and is in his trinity; spirit, soul, body. Man does not have three spirits in himself, one in his spirit, one in his soul, and one in his body, but has one spirit only.

"So is God in whose image we are made. The Father is not the Son, nor is the Holy Spirit the Son - though the three are one; even as man's spirit is not his body nor his soul his body, though the three: spirit, soul, and body make one man.

"The water that gushes out into a living spring may have come from a greater reservoir and may run for a long way through an underground channel, but it is not a different water from that in the reservoir or in the channel.

"The water in the ever unseen reservoir is the Father. The water ever in action and running in the channel is the Holy Spirit. The water coming in view in the spring to refresh the weary is the Son: It is JESUS, the Water of Life."

J. Munro Gibson, M. A.; D. D., in his book "Christianity according to Christ," published m London, England, 1888: "The Fullness of God in Christ," -

"The name of God is that by which He has made Himself known to us, specially in the course of revelation; above all, the two great names of "Jehovah" in the Old Testament and "Jesus" in the New

As to the name of "Jesus," while the sweetness has never been crushed out of it, as it has out of the rich and precious Old Testament name yet it has not been so closely identified with the Divine Being as it ought to have been. In their zeal for personal distinctions in the Holy Trinity, theologians have been too often tempted to forget such passages as these - "No man cometh unto the Father but by Me," "I and my Father are One," "I am the Truth." etc.; and so they have attempted to unfold a knowledge of God apart from His Son Christ Jesus; that is to say, a knowledge of God apart from that Name by which He has made Himself known to us.

"Show us the Father, and it sufficeth us." Consider, then, that in order to meet this reasonable appeal (for, if He be our Father, why should He not show Himself to us?) it is necessary that there should be some visible form; and if some visible form, it needs little consideration to decide which it is likely to be. "He that hath seen Me, hath seen the Father."

The Man Christ Jesus is the face of God to us. By looking at Him we become acquainted with our Father in heaven; not otherwise; "No man cometh unto the Father but by Me."

Here, in the face of Jesus Christ, is "the knowledge of the glory of. God." There is no other possible facility for knowing God. Even at the best and fullest our knowledge will remain but partial and inadequate. It will be far from absolute knowledg

So the whole knowledge of the Father is provided in Christ. We are "complete in Him." From all this it follows that those who would know God must seek Him in Christ

First, it is not the absolute essence of Deity that we are to seek; it is His face, what of Him is turned to us, so that we can see and recognize Him. Hence the prominence given to "the Name of God."

The word "Trinity" does not occur in Scripture, nor is there anything to be found there corresponding to those complicated formulas by which (notably in the so-called Athanasian Creed) theologians have tried to define the relations of Father, Son and Holy Ghost. If theologians had only followed the Scriptures in this respect, how many bitter controversies might have been spared, and how many needless difficulties and perplexities would have been avoided.

"I am the Life," says the Lord Jesus, claiming thus the special prerogative of the Holy Spirit. What Christian minister has not again and again been consulted by good people, who were in some perplexity as to which of the Three Persons of the Trinity they should address themselves to. Some have, even been afraid they might pray too much to one Person and thus create jealousy between them.

"There is no knowledge of the Spirit apart from the knowledge of Christ. In fact, so complete is the identification that the Lord speaks of the Spirit's coming as His own. - John 14.

The presence of Jesus was to be withdrawn in one sense, but restored in another: it was to be withdrawn in an inferior degree, to be restored in a far better way;. it was to be withdrawn after the flesh and restored in the Spirit; it was to be withdrawn as a human presence and restored as a Divine presence; it was to be withdrawn as a local presence, and restored as omnipresence; it was to be withdrawn as an occasional and temporary presence, and restored as a perpetually abiding presence; all of which is implied in the transition from the preposition with to the preposition in.

"No man can say Jesus is Lord, but in the Holy Spirit." We must find a point of vital contact with the Spirit of God, and this is found only in His Son Jesus Christ.

Again and again Jesus speaks of the coming of the Spirit as equivalent to His own coming again to continue the work that He had begun on earth. It was His Spirit that He was speaking of. He ascended to His Father and ours, and His Spirit came to guide the disciples into all truth.

The Bible is not responsible for the formula so generally used of "Three in and One, and One in Three." While God may be said to be Three as well as One, it is certainly never meant that He is or can be Three and One in the same sense.

The Father is presented to our thoughts as God invisible, inaccessible; the Son, as God manifest; the Spirit, as God working. Though the Word is eternal, the Incarnate Word had, a beginning; and though the Spirit is eternal, the indwelling Spirit dates from Pentecost. The Eternal Spirit came as the Spirit of the Son. The Incarnation prepared the way for the Indwelling; the Indwelling crowned the Incarnation by rendering it practically universal and perpetual.

The Incarnate Word and the Indwelling Spirit have almost lost their connection among Christians. "The Comforter," "the Paraclete," is always understood of the Spirit; and it seems rarely to suggest itself to the minds of Christians that the Lord "Jesus" has equal claim to the title.

He who came before as the Spirit of God is now come as the Spirit of the Lord Jesus. His coming is, to all intents and purposes, the coming of the Lord Jesus Himself." "I will not leave you comfortless, I will come to you." "God manifested in the flesh," was "justified in the Spirit." The "only begotten Son," by His atoning death took away the sin of the world, and gave His Holy Spirit.

"At that day ye shall know that I am in the Father, and ye in Me, and I in you." - John 14:20. The Saints of old did not have this knowledge. Nor did the disciples of Christ reach it in the days of His flesh. They had as yet no experience of being in Him, and He in them.

The Father, Son and Holy Ghost are all in Jesus Christ. "I am the Way, the Truth and the Life." Father, Son and Holy Ghost are all here, each found in Him, so that our thoughts are not to leave Christ when they pass to the Father or to the Holy Spirit. Christ is all - in Him dwelleth all the fullness of the Godhead bodily.

Now this is manifestly the way in which we are intended to realize to ourselves the truth about God as Father, as Son, as Holy Spirit - not by wandering away into the infinite, but sitting at the feet of Jesus and looking up into His face.

The reason why some get into difficulty and perplexity is their perverse determination - notwithstanding all the directions and cautions the Master has given - to seek a separate knowledge of the Father, Son and Holy Spirit. They wish to know God the Father, Son and Holy Spirit. They wish to Know God the Father, and in order to find Him, they look away from Christ, instead of at Him. They gaze into the infinite unknown instead of looking at the face of Jesus. And when they think of the Spirit, again they must have this as a separate region of theological lore.

So again they look away from the face of Jesus to find somewhere else God the Holy Spirit. If they would have what they are vainly seeking, they would have three Gods instead of one, as practically many Christians have, for they actually have great difficulty sometimes as to which of the three to go to.

It is very easy to show how utterly needless all this perplexity is, and how thoroughly unscriptural are all these notions out of which it grows. There is only one Person, to whom any one can go, and, that Person is Christ. We should go to Him always, under all circumstances, with our prayers, with our tears, with our longings, with our doubts, with our difficulties, with our troubles, with our innumerable wants.

When we say "Our Father," we must look to Christ, for He plainly tells us that we cannot reach the Father but by Him. Christ Himself says, as plainly as tongue can express it, that it's impossible to know the Father apart from Him. "No man, cometh unto the Father but by Me." And when even after that plain statement the still puzzled disciple says, "Lord, show us the Father, and it sufficeth us," what can the Master do but repeat the same truth in still more emphatic terms, "He that hath seen Me hath seen the Father." Do you not know Me yet? Who can suppose that Philip retained his perplexity after so clear an answer? Why should any one be perplexed now?

Christ is the only way, and those who turn away from Him set their faces to the outer darkness. The same considerations apply to those who perplex and confuse themselves by trying to have a knowledge of the Spirit apart from their knowledge of Christ. Our Savior claims, Himself to be the Life, as well as the Truth.

He speaks of the giving of "another Comforter," but, when He comes He will not speak of Himself, but "He shall take of the things of Mine and show it unto you". So complete is their identification that the Lord speaks of His coming as His own coming: "I will not leave you comfortless; I will come to you." "At that day ye shall know that I am in the Father, and ye in Me, and I in you."

"I am in the Father" - there is the doctrine of the Father. "Ye in Me" - there is the doctrine of the Son. "I in you" - there is the doctrine of the Spirit. If we think of the Father, there is Christ - "I am in the Father, and the Father in Me." If we think of the Son, union to Christ is the practical thought - "ye in Me." If we think of the Holy Spirit, the practical thought is Christ in us - "I in you."

It comes to this, that practically Christ is all in all. "I am the Way, the Truth and the Life." It is "I am" all the way through. The divine name is all in Christ. "Hear, O Israel ! The Lord our God is one Lord." The unsearchable God has made Himself known to us as Father, Son and Holy Spirit. But all that there is for us in the Father - all that there is for us in the Son - all that there is for us in the Holy Spirit - is manifest in Christ.

He is all and in all. All praise and glory to Christ the Son - the only Revealer of the Father - the only Fountain of the Spirit. Let our prayers always be to Him, whether we are looking at the Father as revealed in Him, or whether we are looking at Him, as the source whence flow the streams of the Spirit's life.

Whether we are thinking of the invisible God quite out of our reach, or the invisible Spirit proceeding from Him and entering into us, the eye of faith is ever directed to Him who is for us the face of God. "God, who commanded the light to shine out of darkness, hath shined in our hearts, to give the light of the knowledge of the glory of God in the face of Jesus Christ."

Light shining out of darkness suggests the Father; shining in our hearts suggests the Spirit; shining reflected from the face of Jesus Christ - there is the Son. There is only one face to look at - only one direction for the eye to take. All is simple as when one speaks to a friend." - J. Munro Gibson.

Mrs. J. Penn-Lewis: "Now for a moment pass on to Acts 2, and read it in the light of John 14:20; for, as we have seen, it is the Lord's foreshadowing of what would occur to the disciples inwardly when the Holy Ghost came down, and filled the house where they were sitting. The disciples knew as the Spirit of God came, that Christ was God in very truth, that the Man they had seen go up into heaven had reached the unseen Father, and was, as He had said, "In the Father" - one with Him. Very God of very God."

Carl M. Nichelsen, in Pentecostal Evangel": "God allows no man to become familiar' with Him. Some are daring enough to attempt to put God under their mental microscope in order to determine the make-up of His character, and, measure the mighty Jehovah by their intellectual tape lines, and other human standards. At the very sight of the Almighty, the breath of man would instantly leave him. God must be known some other way, by revelation to man's inner consciousness. Although God has outwardly manifested Himself at times, His Deity was always veiled. Even in the case of the outer manifestation of God, through Jesus Christ, to Saul on the way to Damascus, the sight blinded him and struck him to the ground."

Sunday School Times, July 30, 1921: "Look unto me and be ye saved." - Isa. 45:18-24. Compare v. 22, with John 1:29. The Jehovah of the Old Covenant is the Jesus of the New. The two are one. The Jews' Jehovah is the world's Savior."

Some one has written the following facts on the Memorial Name: "Elohim in its first occurrence connects it, with creation, and gives it its essential meaning as the Creator. Elohim is God, the living God, the power of creation. (John 1:3, Col. 1:15-17, Rev. 3:14; 4:11.) He first assumes a creature form, though spiritual in nature (Gen. 12:7; 32:24-30, Isa. 6:1-5), afterwards the human form, for the purpose of redeeming mankind. (John 1:14, Heb. 2:9, 14, 16, 17, Phil. 2:7, Rom. 8:3.) That Elohim, in His creature form spiritually, who appeared to the patriarchs and prophets, is the same who appeared in a human form 1900 years ago to Israel, can be clearly seen by the following Scriptures: Gen. 17:1-3, Ex. 6:2, 3, with John 8;56-58, Isa. 6:1-8, with John 12:41-45.

"Jehovah: "While Elohim is God as the Creator of all things, Jehovah is the same God in covenant relation to those whom He has created, Jehovah means the Eternal, the Immutable One; He who was, and is, and is to come. - Gen. 21:33. He is especially, therefore, the God of Israel; and the God of those who are redeemed, and are thus now "in Christ."

"The Jehovah Titles: "Jehovah-Jireh. - Gen. 22:14. Jehova-Ropheka. - Ex. 15:26. Jehovah-Nissi. - Ex. 17:15. Jehovah-Mekaddishkem - Ex. 31:13. Jehovah-Shalom - Judges 6:24, Jehovah-Zabaoth. - I Sam'l 1:3, etc. Jehovah-Zidkenu. - Jer. 23:6. Jehovah-Shammah. - Ezek. 48:25. Jehovah Elyon. - Ps. 7:17. Jehovah-Roi. - Ps. 23:1. Jah is Jehovah in a special sense and relation. Jehovah as having become our salvation - Ps 68:4, (Ex 15:2).

"Which of these names and titles, with their meanings, do we not find incorporated in the Name of Jesus, The Psalmist declared, "Thou East magnified thy Word above all thy name." - Ps. 138:2. "In the beginning was the Word, and the Word was with God, and the Word was God. And the Word became flesh." John 1:1,14. "His name shall be called Jesus." - Matt. 1:21-23. And He has been given "a name which is above every name" - Eph. 1:21-23, Phil. 2:9.

"When Jacob wrestled with the angel he sought to obtain the secret name, but was prohibited. - Gen. 32:29. When Moses sought to obtain the secret name, all that he received from the angel in the burning bush was, "I am that I am." - Ex. 3:14. The Children of Israel were led by the Angel of the Lord, and Jehovah said, "Beware of him; for my name is in him." - Ex. 23:21. To Manoah, the Jehovah Angel replied, "Why askest thou after my name, seeing it is secret (Wonderful)." - Judges 13:8. The prophet Isaiah declared, "His name shall be called Wonderful" - Isa. 9:6. From these Scriptures it can be clearly seen that Jehovah had a name to be revealed which was to be above all His names. - Matt. 1:20. 21.

"When the Angel appeared to the Virgin in Nazareth, it was there that he finished his journey over the hills of time and deposited that "secret name" in the bosom of her who was "highly favored" of God. - Matt. 1:20; 21, Luke 1:26-31, "His name shall be called JESUS." All the titles that Jehovah ever bore are comprehended in this one name, JESUS. The name of "Jesus" bears in it all that God's other names ever bore. All the attributes of God, as revealed by His names, are found in Jesus. - Rev. 1:8, Ex. 6:3. "For in Him dwelleth all the fullness of the Godhead bodily, and ye are complete in Him." - Col. 2:9, 10, Col. 1:17. In the Book of Acts the whole battle raged around "the Name." "and hast not denied my name." - Rev. 3:8.

"God is one. None apart from Him, none equal with Him; none beside Him; none formed after Him; none like Him, and none with Him. Jesus Christ is the manifestation of that one God in the flesh."

Sunday School Times, "Thou art not yet 50 years old, and hast thou seen Abraham? Jesus said unto them, Before Abraham was I am." - John 8:57, 58. Jesus was claiming that He existed in the eternity of the past. He was claiming for Himself one of the O. T. titles of Jehovah. It was as though He had said that it was Himself that was spoken of by Moses in Ex. 3:14. "I Am" describes Jehovah as the ever existent One, "who was, and is, and is to come." ("Jesus Christ the same yesterday, and today, and forever." - Heb. 13:8.) Jesus was He. "He is before all things, and in Him all things consist." - Col. 1:17..

Another writer has said: "They (most christians) do not have the full apostolic vision of Jesus Christ as Lord or Jehovah. "All" the fullness of the Godhead is in Jesus Christ. - Col. 2:9. Don't be afraid the Father and the Holy Ghost will be left out. "He that hath seen me hath seen the Father." - John 14:7-10; 10:30, 38; 12:44, 45; 17:10. "He that confesseth the Son hath the Father also." - I John 2:23, 24, R. V.; 4:15.

The Deity of Christ

"It is unreasonable when magnifying Jesus as Lord to stop and mystify the readers on the Greek mysteries about the Trinity. Few after years of study know much more about it than when they began. I never knew of any one being saved by a study of the Trinity, but exalting Jesus Christ as the mighty Lord, able to save to the uttermost, will do it.

"No man can come to God except through Christ, and he that has the Christ or Son, "hath the Father also." They are inseparable. You can't get Christ without getting the Father also, even if you want to. God gives Himself only in the Son. Also whoever gets Christ in His fulness gets the Holy Ghost also. "In that day (Pentecost) ye shall know that I am in my Father, and ye in me, and I in you." - John 14:20, 23.

"There was a mysterious angel called the angel of the Lord, that went before the camp of Israel which was none other than Christ the Lord - Jehovah in Angelic form. - Ex. 3:2-14; 14:9; 23:20, 21, (Isa. 42:8), Acts 2:36, Phil. 2:9-11, I Cor. 15:47, I Cor. 3:17. So the whole Godhead in all its fulness is in Jesus.

"The apostles started the church out right with the vision of Jesus as "the Lord from heaven." "God is Spirit." - John 4:24. "Now the Lord is that Spirit" - II Cor. 3:17." E. N. B..

"Bishop Hippolytus, born in the latter part of the second century, a disciple of Iraneaus: "Let us believe then, according to the tradition of the apostles, that God the Word came down from Heaven, and entered the holy Virgin Mary. The Father is one whose Word is present with Him, by whom He made all things. Whom also the Father sent forth in later times for the salvation of men. He now coming forth into the world, was manifested as God in a body.

"Thus then, though demonstrated as God, He does not refuse the condition proper to Him as man. He who as God has a sleepless nature, slumbers on a pillow. In agony He sweats blood, and is strengthened by an angel, who Himself strengthens those who believe on Him. He who is inseparable from the Father, cries to the Father and commends to Him His spirit; and bowing His head He gives up the ghost, who said "I have power to lay down my life, and I have power to take it again." - John 19:18. And because He was not overmastered by death, as being Himself life, He said thus: "I lay it down of myself." He who raises the dead is wrapped in linen and laid in a sepulchre, and on the third day is raised again by the Father, though Himself the resurrection and the life. For all these things He has finished for us; who for our sakes was made as we are, except sin. This is the God who for our sakes became man; to whom also the Father hath put all things in subjection.

E. N. Bell, in "The Truth about the Godhead": "It was no use for Philip to ask any other revelation of the Father. The Father is seen by seeing Jesus. He that has seen Jesus has seen all of the Father that the Father intends now to reveal. No true Trinitarian can logically deny the Deity of Jesus as the Son of God. To do so is to make him a mere created being like ourselves. Those who should worship such a created being would be pure idolators. God forbids us worshipping anything less than Himself. We cannot worship Jesus unless He is truly God. The Arians believed that Jesus was a little less than God, yet higher than the noblest angel, and still worshipped Him.

"The Scriptures clearly teach that He is God. - Isa. 9:6, "Mighty God." Heb. 1:8, "Thy throne, O God is forever and ever." John 20:28, "My Lord and My God," - (Rom. 9:5), It is an unspeakable joy to ascribe unto the Son all the attributes of Deity. We need not expect as finite beings to understand fully the mysteries in the Being of the Infinite God. No intelligent Trinitarian believes there are three material or corporeal bodies in the Godhead. Jesus is the only one in the Godhead who has a material and glorified body. The Latin word (persona) from which we get our word person has absolutely nothing in it even suggesting a material body.

"These three persons (of the Godhead) are not three gods. Because they coexist, in one divine essence, in one divine nature, they constitute one God, and His name is one. We have not gods many and lords many, as the heathen. We all believe that our Lord Jesus Christ is truly God. If Jesus is God at all, as we all believe He is of course He is the true God, not a false God. We love and adore Jesus as our Lord and our God. He is the only way to the Father, the way of Life. "Whosoever denieth the Son, the same hath not the Father; but he that acknowledgeth the Son, hath the Father also," - John 2:23." - E. N. Bell. Now if this latter statement be true, and it is the Word, then how foolish to talk about denying the Father. We have both the Father and the Son.

CHAPTER IV

W. Graham Scroggie, in "Sunday School Times," Col. 1:15-17, - God the Father is eternally hidden and unknowable, - Col. 1:15, Ex. 33:20, Matt. 11:27, John 1:18; 6:46. I Tim. 1:17; 6:15, 16, - No man by searching can find out God. Direct and immediate knowledge of Him is impossible. He is the "invisible" and, therefore, the unknowable God.

In Christ the invisible God is fully and finally revealed. In Christ God becomes visible and all things else become intelligible. "He that hath seen me hath seen the Father." - John 14:9. Heb. 1:3, - The Son is "the effulgence of God's glory, and the very image of His substance." He is the manifestation of the divine attributes, and the embodiment of the divine essence. In Him the glory of God is radiated, and His character reflected. He makes visible the "invisible." The essentially invisible Father has in the Son an eternal organ of self-manifestation. ("God is Spirit.")

The incarnation of Christ was not the beginning of His "exegesis" of "the invisible God." That began away back in the remoteness of eternity. Christ is God, without beginning, supreme, and transcendent. This was His own consciousness in incarnate life. There would be no need for God to be revealed if there were no intelligences (creatures) outside of the Godhead to behold Him; and speculatively one may say that, but for such intelligences, Christ would never have become "the image of the invisible God." - (and become man.)

If Christ be not God He cannot be either Creator or Redeemer. Christ is not merely like God, but is God, and therefore pre-existent and uncreated, absolute in His eternity. - Phil. 2:6. Christ is the originator of all things. "In him were all things created." - Col. 1:16, 17. All things were created by Christ and for Him. Christ is the controller of all things. "In him all things consist." Christ is as certainly at work in nature and in history as in His church. Back of both is the divine Thinker, the infinite Wisdom, the almighty Power, who is the Son of God and our Redeemer, in Whom all things have their center of unity, who appoints to everything its place, who determines the relation of things to one another, and who combines all into an ordered whole so that this universe is a cosmos and not a chaos.

Christ is the perfecter of all things. Not only is He the Origin, and the Head, but also the Goal of the whole universe; the creative Cause, the continuous Cause, and the consummating Cause of all things. The world advances towards the fulfilment of its destiny in God through Christ. The time is sure when all things shall be summed up in Him. - Eph. 1:10.

By Christ the Father's purpose passes into actuality and attains its end. He who is the Agent of creation is also its Aim, the Starting-point is also the Goal, the Alpha is also the Omega, the First is also the Last; that which proceeded from Christ and is sustained by Him also converges toward Him. The Creator and Redeemer is the Perfecter of all things. We should ever endeavor to see in one view the eternal Christ, and the historical Christ, the Creator and the Redeemer, not two persons but one. - Edinburg, Scotland.

Rev. C. H. Pridgeon has written: "The word "person" is inadequate when referring to the Godhead: Father, Son, and Holy Spirit. Augustine, Calvin, and others express their regret at having to use so imperfect and misleading a word; but it was the best known word they had or we have. The words "subsistence" or "hypostasis," are more accurate, but are too little understood. There are three such subsistences or hypostases in the Godhead and the Three make One. There is but one tree, not three. God the Father is the root, the Hidden God: God the Son is the part of the tree above the ground, He is the Manifest God: and the Holy Spirit is the Life that flows from one into the other and then outward. Again, God the Father may be compared to a great Love-Fire, which eternally begets the Son, who is the Light: and the Holy Spirit is the heat and chemical rays that proceed from both.

"In man desire generates images and thoughts. In God such generations are eternal realities. In His Deity the Son of God is uncreated: in His humanity He was created.

"Then cometh the end, when He shall have delivered up the kingdom to God, even the Father; . . . And when all things shall be subdued unto Him, then shall the Son also Himself be subject unto Him that put all things under Him, that God may be all in all." - I Cor. 15:24-28; The reign of Christ, as Son of Man and Redeemer, comes to an end when His work of redemption is completed at the end of the ages. Then all things are subject to Him and He hands over all to the Father and He

Himself has no more redeeming work to do as Son of Man, but in that capacity becomes subject to the Father. It might be well to notice that although the Son of Man becomes subject to the Father, the Scripture does not say that the Father becomes "all in all," but "God (becomes) may be all in all," that is, the whole Godhead becomes "all in all." Christ as Redeemer and Son of Man becomes subject; but as Son of God He part of the Godhead that becomes all and in all. The Son will hand over the perfected kingdom to the Father, and God (Father, Son, and. Holy Ghost) will be "all in all."

S. A. Jamison, in "Bridegroom's Messenger: "In this age of modernistic teaching, especially when Jesus Christ is robbed of His Deity, it is very essential for the christian to have a clear idea of the Trinity. In the Godhead the three persons are the same in substance, of one and the same indivisible essence. This divine essence as a whole exists eternally as Father, and as Son, and as the Holy Ghost. Each person possesses the whole essence. The Son is eternally begotten by the Father. The Son is not from the Father, but in the Father, and the Father in the Son. The Spirit proceedeth from the Father and the Son. Christ has existed from eternity as the coequal Son of the Father, possessing the same self-existent essence with the Father and the Holy Ghost."

"Some one has said that we should read the Bible only from one standpoint, to know the Lord Jesus Christ; and if one studies the Bible for any other purpose he will not understand it. The Bible begins with Jesus (Gen. 3:15), and ends with Him. In fact it is a revelation of Jesus Christ. The revelation of "God in Christ" - II Cor. 5:19. Christ is not only the central figure of the Bible, but the "First and the Last." - Rev. 1:8; 22:13, Isa. 41:4; 43:10.

H. L. Hastings, Editor of "The Christian," once wrote the following: "In those old days, when men whose kingdom was "of this world," and whose servants were therefore willing to fight, had assumed authority over the flock of God, and had established organizations in which politics was more potent than piety, and where faith, instead of coming by hearing, and hearing by the Word of God, was settled by the decisions of councils and the decrees of despots; when men disputed about things they did not understand, and persecuted people who chanced to know more or less than they did, etc."

From the Encyclopedia Brittanica, on "The Council of Nicae, 325 A. D., we read: "Ecumenical Councils were called and controlled by the State, the Emperor. The expenses were largely paid, the delegates appointed, by the Emperor. Emperor Constantine appointed the time and place for the Council of Nicae, summoned the episcopate, paid part of the expense out of the public purse, nominated the committee in charge of the order of business, used his influence to bring about the adoption of the creed, and punished those who refused to subscribe. This council was no more an organ of ecclesiastical self-government than were the synods of Rome and Arles. It was rather a means whereby the church was ruled by secular power. The final goal of Greek philosophy was only reached when the great thinkers of the early christian church, who had been trained in the schools of Alexandria and Athens, used its modes of thought in their analysis of the christian idea of God. The result was the evolution of the doctrine of the Trinity."

The fact is the Emperor Constantine only submitted to christian baptism on his death bed. He was afraid of forfeiting salvation before this, on account of his sins, which he had no desire to relinquish.

Some one has reflected as follows on this subject: "Why did not the saints in the second and third centuries cling to the great names of their Lord (in the Word), and find in Him all the mysteries connected with the Godhead? But instead of doing this some began to preach from the philosophy of Rome, Egypt, and Babylon, by which they tried to explain the Godhead. Hence Sabellianism, Arianism, and Athanasianism, the outcome of which was, and is today, a furious battle among God's people. Oh that we would endeavor to keep the unity of the Spirit in the bond of peace, and at once throw all these isms into the garbage can, clinging to the prophetic and apostolic teaching, magnifying the Father in the person and name of the Son, by the power and the love of the Holy Spirit, seeing and preaching the fullness of the Godhead in the Lord Jesus Christ, according to the Scripture." And I say, Amen ! ! !

St. Bernard: "When I name Christ Jesus I set before myself a Man meek and lowly of heart, conspicuous by all moral dignity and holiness, and One who is at the same time God Almighty, to heal me by His example, and to strengthen me by His aid."

St. Chrysostom: "Christ is not valued at all unless He is valued above all. When thou hearest of Christ, do not think Him God only, or man only, but both together."

The following beautiful poem, author unknown, we give in prose, to economize space: "Our Lord Jesus Christ." - "Thou art Alpha and Omega, Living Word, of men the Light. Son of God, the Well Beloved, Source of Heaven's great delight. Everlasting Father, Dayspring, Smitten Rock, Foundation Sure. Thou art laid elect and precious, as the Cornerstone secure.

"Lion of the Tribe of Judah, Israel's Sceptre rising strong. Branch of David, Root of Jesse, Great Messiah promised long. Son of Man, Jehovah's Servant, Glory of the Chosen Race. Faithful

Witness, Prophet, Shepherd, Thou host Thy law enlarged through Grace.

"Man of Sorrows, Galilean, Nazarene, despised, oppressed. Bread of Life, with body broken, open Door to peace and rest. O Immanuel, the Holy, God, indeed, with us Thou art. Jesus, Savior, great Redeemer, Bleeding Lamb with broken heart.

"First Born from the dead, we hail thee, Resurrection and the Life. Heir of all things, Thou hast conquered, through the grim and awful strife. Thou the Church's Head, all glorious, art the Lord our Righteousness. Wonderful, we laud, adore Thee, Mighty God, thy name we bless.

"Vine supporting many branches, Lily of the Valley fair. Chiefest One among Ten Thousand, Sharon's Rose of beauty rare. Altogether Lovely, Bridegroom, Faithful, True, our Advocate. Bishop of our Souls, so tender, evermore our High-Priest great."

Rev. A. C. Dixon, D. D.: "A child shall be born, a son shall be given, and he shall be called the Wonderful, the Counsellor, the Mighty God, the Everlasting Father, the Prince of Peace." - (Isa. 9:6.) The birth Jesus was therefore the incarnation of Deity. When we think of God we are apt to think of Him in human form. God revealed Himself to Joshua and others in human form.

"Jesus was the Son of Man; not a Son of Man. The blood of the whole race was in His veins. There is a universality in the character of Christ which you find in no other man. There is nothing of nationality in Him. There is nothing peculiar to any particular age of the world in Him. His was a heart pulsating with the blood of the human race.

"Jesus taught that He was God. "He that hath seen me hath seen the Father." - John 14:9John 14:9, "He that seeth me seeth Him that sent me." - John 12:45. His mission was to manifest God in His own person. "God was manifest in the flesh." - I Tim. 3:16. Jesus taught the impossibility of knowing God the Father except through Himself. "No man knoweth the Father save the Son, and he to whomsoever the Son will reveal Him" - Matt. 11:27. He claims identity of divine nature with the Father. "I and my (the) Father are one." - John 10:30. He calmly claims attributes which none but God can possess. He declares that He is eternal. "Before Abraham was, I am." - John 8:58. He claims to be omnipresent as to place and time. "Where two or three are gathered together in my name, there am I in the midst of them" - Matt. 18:20. "Lo, I am with you alway, even unto the end of the world." - Matt. 28:20.

"Jesus taught that He was God, and John crowns Him Creator of the universe. - John 1:3. "This is the true God (Christ) and eternal life." - I John 5:20. Paul's Christ "who is over all God blessed forever," (Rom. 9:5), is the true Christ. Jesus Christ was either deceived, madman, a bad man, or God. He was either God or the worst of men. We have just seen that He claimed the attributes of Deity. "Why callest thou me good, there is none good, but one, that is God." - Mark 10:17, 18. To say that I am good is equal to saying that I am God. All admit that He is good; and if good, He is God. Christ was more than man, and as I see Him standing out distinct from and above all others, I cannot resist the impulse to fall at His feet and say with Thomas, "My Lord and my God." - A. C. Dixon.

Another writer has said: "It is strange that people would look beyond the Lord Jesus Christ in an attempt to find the unknown God. The fountain proper comes forth from the unseen fountain head, and yet never ceases to be a part of it. The fountain proper is merely the fountain head in action. Therefore Jesus could say, "I and my (the) Father are one." He could be called at the same time "the Only begotten of the Father," and the very God Himself. "Emmanu-El." - Matt. 1:23. Jude 24:25, I John 5:20. Jesus represents the entire person of God. He is all I need." - (I Cor. 1:30.)

"We should never attempt to explain the mystery of God's person by mere human wisdom. The Lord Jesus Christ was the complete solution to the mystery of God's person. "He that hath seen me hath seen the Father." Is not our Lord great enough to fill our vision? Is He not sufficiently full of mystery to invite all of our thoughts and meditations to Himself? Let us hail Him as Thomas did, "My Lord and my God." "Of whom we have many things to say, and hard to be uttered, seeing ye are dull of hearing." - Heb. 5:11. "Unto the measure of the stature of the fulness of Christ." - Eph. 4:13. (We can never be disappointed in Him. - Eph. 1:10; 3:17-19.)

Prof. Frederick S. Jewell, Ph. D.: "Amid whatever changes of arts, letters, institutions and empires, one figure continues supreme in history. It is that of the man John baptized, whom Pilate crucified; who built no capital, led no army, wrote no wrote no volume; who seemed yet to the principal persons of his time to have fitly closed a restless yet an obscure life in ignoble death; but who named Himself, and who now is named in all the written languages of mankind, the Son of God and God Almighty."

Neander: "The God who dwells in a light inaccessible into which the human spirit cannot penetrate must descend to humanity, bringing Himself into the limits of Man's own finiteness in order to be truly known by him. Not until the incarnate manifestation of Deity through Christ, could the God afar off draw near mankind. For the first time, through this image of the Divine in human nature, was the idea of God enabled to enter in a vital and substantial way, into the thought and consciousness of the human race.

Zachary Eddy, D. D.: Let us not think of Christ as a man created by divine power, and then taken into intimate union with God - not as God and man morally - but as GOD-MAN, the true holy of holies wherein God personally dwells, and will dwell henceforth, even forever. There is the Well-Spring of life for a dead world; there is the light of men, the Son of truth and wisdom; there, is the image of the invisible God, and the brightness of His glory; there, is the Lord God our Redeemer, the Holy One of Israel, the Savior. Yes, we adore Thee, Son of the Virgin, Son of God. Seeing Thee we see the Father. We worship Thee, in whom God is become man and man is taken into God.

"Messenger of the Kingdom": "Alpha and Omega are A to Z of the Greek language. Jesus said, "I am Alpha and Omega." He expressed Himself actually to be the whole written Word. The biggest and greatest revelation of the Eternal God and His mysterious, majestic person is the good old Bible. The God which we find in the sacred pages of the Bible is the true God. Since Jesus is our written and spiritual Bible, and the true God is found in the Bible, then it remains for us to look in the person and name and the sayings of our blessed Lord to find and know and worship the true God. The central theme of the Word of God is "God in Christ Jesus." Therefore, we see our blessed Alpha and Omega in Genesis, and all the way through to the Book of Revelation."

"The Pentecostal Evangel": "The name Lord or Jehovah is pre-eminently God's redemption name. It is used in Bible passages which specifically refer to the redeeming and saving work that God does for fallen, sinful man. Jehovah God, our Redeemer God, in His marvelous covenant relations with us, is the Eternal Christ, slain from the foundation of the world, whose outpoured life is the grace of God, working omnipotently in our behalf."

Dr. Wm. L. Pettingill, Pres't of Phila. Bible School: "All christians will one day be fundamentalists. That day will be when we get to heaven. Only those who believe in Christ as God, in His virgin birth, and in his resurrection - an irreducible minimum of christian faith - will go to heaven. Those who deny this will be lost and go to hell." This would surely be a bad line-up for Pentecostal people.

Dr. Campbell Morgan says: "When Jesus told the young ruler there was "none good but one - God," He meant to declare that He Himself was God. - Matt. 19:17.

Rev. Elijah Hedding, in a Sermon preached before the Annual Meth. Conf., at Bath, Maine, in 1822, made the following statements, with a host of ample Scripture reference to prove his assertions. We have only room for the statements. " John 1:1, 2, - Of the word it is here affirmed He is God. Jesus Christ is the Supreme God. Father and Son are one and the same Being. Christ is the true God, and Eternal Life. Christ is God over all. Jesus Christ is the Lord God of the holy Prophets. Jesus is Jehovah. Christ is the One Eternal Supreme Being. Christ is the Immutable Being. Christ Omniscient Being. Christ is the Omnipresent Being. Christ is the Almighty Being. Christ is the proper Object of worship. Christ is the Creator of all things. God and the Word are the same Being." This was the belief and teaching of Early Methodism.

James Speirs, London, England: "All christians believe that Jesus is the Son of God, the Lamb of God, an Advocate with God, and a Mediator between God and Man. But the higher truths in relation to His Divinity are entirely overlooked. The Sonship of Jesus is admitted. He is regarded as the Lamb of God. But not as God Himself. The confession that Jesus is God is merely verbal; the feeling that He is a being inferior and subordinate is inrooted. The Jehovah God of the O. T. is the Jesus Christ of the N. T. Jesus is God Himself, Creator and Sustainer of the world that came in flesh and dwelt in it a while. Jehovah and Jesus are one." (Luke 13:34, 35, Ps. 91:14.)

Some one has written: "The apostles saw Jesus as God and manifest in the flesh, as the One by whom and for whom all things were created, and as the new Sinless Head of the whole human race; and they saw aright. In the present awful apostasy the time seems to be right to call for a world-wide and final answer to a challenge like that given by Elijah to the people of Israel on Mt. Camel long ago. That challenge takes this form, "If Jesus Christ be God, follow Him."

L. T. Townsend: "If John believed that Jesus Christ was united to Deity, in such manner as to be God's real Personality, he could have expressed himself in no other way so briefly, so directly, so clearly and so well as to say, "In the beginning was the Word, and the Word was with God, and the Word was God." - John 1:1. Rev. 3:1; 15:3; 17:4.

"It must be clear to all that Jesus Christ, in John's Christology is the God whose glory Isaiah saw in the vision, when it filled the temple and shook its foundations - Isa. 6:1-5, John 12:41. He is Alpha and Omega. - Rev. 22:13. The true God. - I John 5:20.

Jesus in the Scriptures is called God, or by a name implying it, no less than 15 times. Seventy-seven times He is called Lord; ten times are the same things spoken of Him as God; and 52 times He is presented as an object of worship. 15 as possessing eternal life; in 17 as Judge of the world; in 20 as the bestower of rewards; and in 24 as the executor of the punishment of the wicked.

The Jews clearly understood Him to teach that He was God. It was for this claim that they attempted to kill Him. This to them was blasphemy, and it was blasphemy unless He possessed and could wield all the attributes of Jehovah. When we mass all these facts must we not say that Jesus felt beyond a doubt that there was in Him an essential substance which in no respect differs from Deity?"

"The Wonderful Word": "Jesus Christ is no less than the God-man, and the one in whom all the fullness of the Godhead dwells. He is the greatest Person in the universe. There is no place high enough, for he fills all things. Human language does not contain words sufficient to tell of His worth. Words utterly break fail and break down in attempt to give Him honor, Who is above all, over all, and in all. Vowels, consonants and dipthongs cannot unite the framing words that speak of His matchless glory. "Christ is the Fact of facts, the Bible's Theme. He is the God, all Light from Him doth gleam. He is the Man of men, beyond all dream. He is the God of love, all love Divine. He's All! The Visibility of God."

"The Incarnation is called "the mystery of godliness." As the Cherubim bent in reverent perplexity over the Ark of the Covenant, so do we devoutly ponder this fundamental truth. The angels desire to look into it. - I Peter 1:12.

Adam Clarke, on I Cor. 15:27, 28: "He is excepted," i.e., the Father; who hath put all things under him, the Son. This observation seems to be introduced by the apostle to show, that he does not mean that the Divine Nature shall be subject to the human nature. Christ, as Messiah, and Mediator between God and Man, must be considered inferior to the Father; and his human nature, however dignified in consequence of its union with the Divine Nature, must be inferior to God. The whole of this verse should be read in a parenthesis.

"The Son also himself shall be subject." Then the administration of the kingdom of grace is finally closed; when there shall be no longer any state of probation; and consequently no longer need a distinction between the kingdom of grace, and the kingdom of glory; then the Son, as being man, shall cease to exercise any distinct dominion; and God be all in all; there remaining no longer any distinction in the persons of the glorious Trinity, as acting any distinct or separate parts in either the kingdom of grace, or the kingdom of glory; and so the one infinite essence shall appear undivided and eternal." - Clarke.

Bishop Lightfoot, on Phil. 2:6: "The form of God" means the "essential attributes of God."

Rev. L..W.: Gosnell, Assis. Dean, Moody Bible Inst., quoting B. B. Warfield, says: "The form of God' is the sum of the characteristics which make the being we call God, specifically God, rather than some other being, - an angel, say, or a man. When our Lord is said to be in the form of God,' therefore, He is declared, in the most express manner possible to be all that God is, to possess the whole fulness of attributes which make God God."

Bob Shuler: "As to Christ, He was and is either God, or He was and is a liar, for He said He was God."

"The Redeemed Hebrew": "Does not Dr. Isaac Lesser translate Isa. 9:6, as follows, "Counsellor of the Mighty God, of the Everlasting Father," etc.? Lesser renders it so, but he had an object in so doing. It was his intention to distinctly obliterate the most powerful pre-designation of the coming Messiah. In the first place, Lesser does not believe in the Messiah, and in the second place, it was his wish that no one should apply this passage to a Messiah in whom he himself did not believe. The Yiddish translation, and all English, Greek, and other translations give it that the Messiah was to be "The Mighty God, the Everlasting Father," etc. Dr. Torrey, in a sermon on "The Deity of Christ," at The Bible Institute, Los Angeles, some years ago, condemned this translation of Dr. Lesser's on Isa. 9:6.

"The Friend of Russia: "The titles given to Jehovah in the Word of God clearly set forth who and what He is in Himself, His character, nature and eternal Godhead, and also, what He was to His ancient people the chosen race of Israel. But these titles also have a direct application to Christ. Nothing is more clearly taught in the Word of God, than that the Jehovah of the O. T. is the Christ of the N. T., and the Christ of the N. T. is the Jehovah of the O. T. The: O. T. titles of Jehovah assert and proclaim the Deity of the Lord Jesus Christ. Christ is God."

Another well known preacher, at one time head of the Christian Missionary Alliance has recently called attention to the fact that Jehovah, the "I Am," the Logos, the Lord Jesus Christ, was the past, present and future of God. Hence all of God. He was the form God took to reveal Himself to man, so we could know Him. This preacher expressed his conviction that this Jehovah-Jesus is the only God we will ever see.

What a contrast are these expressions to that of a recent teacher in our midst who writes as follows: "Our Christianity has become a Jesus religion, and it is no wonder that strange and fantastic creeds have grown out of It." He declares we are all orphans because of this fact. Possibly forgetting that Jesus Himself said, "I will not leave you "orphans"; I will come unto you." - John 14:18. "He that hath seen me hath seen the Father." - John 14:7-9. "I and the Father are one." - John 10:30. Some have foolishly asked the question, "Is Jesus then his own Father?", thinking thus to dispose of these sublime declarations. The whole trouble with our treatment of this subject is the fact that we have tried to reduce the Godhead to human analogy, reasoning humanly of the nature of the Deity of Christ and the relationship of the Godhead.

Millions of the devoted dupes of Rome hail "the man of sin" as "our Lord God the Pope." Should christians refuse equal homage to our Lord Jesus Christ? The Antichrist will soon set himself forth in the temple "as God." - I John 5:20. Antichrist is "against Christ." It is Christ or Antichrist. Which one shall be God? If Christ, then follow Him. One or the other must be God.

Too many christians, like Philip, are still looking for the Father apart from Christ. They are still begging to be shown the Father. "Doest thou not know me, Philip? "He that hath see me hath seen the Father." - John 14:9. When the Father gave His Son He gave Himself also. We have no Father apart from Jesus. Tradition would have us running up and down stairs in the Ark, trying to find God. But Jesus is the Ark. We are safe in Him. Though there are three stories, there was only one Ark. "That we might know him that is true; and we are in him that is true, in His Son Jesus Christ. He is the true God, and eternal life." - I John 5:20. Dr. Torrey, with most capable Bible students, applies this Scripture to Jesus. Jesus is the very unoriginated God. - John 1:1; 20:28, Acts 20:28, Rom. 9:5, Col. 2:9, Phil 2:6, I Tim. 3:16, Titus 2:10, Heb. 1:8.

"Unto a dispensation of the fullness of times, to sum up all things in Christ." - Eph. 1:10. "Take heed lest there shall be any one that maketh spoil of you through his philosophy and vain deceit, after the tradition of men, and not after Christ, for in Him dwelleth all the fullness of the Godhead bodily, and ye are complete in Him." - Col. 2:8-10. All we can know of the Sun is what reaches our earth. So all we can know of God is what is revealed to us, or reaches us, through and in Jesus Christ.

"That the God of our Lord Jesus Christ, the Father of glory, may give unto you a spirit of wisdom and revelation in the knowledge of him (Christ)." - Eph. 1:17. "Searching what time or what manner of time the Spirit of Christ which was in them (the prophets) did point unto." - I Peter 1:11. "That they may know the mystery of God, Christ, in whom are all the treasures of wisdom and knowledge hidden." - Col. 2:2, 3. "To give the light of the knowledge of the glory of God in the face of Jesus Christ." - II Cor. 4:6.

CHAPTER V

For there are three that bear record in heaven: the Father, the Word, and the Holy Ghost; and these three are one." - I John 5:7. (The Spirit, water and the blood "agree in one," are "to the point." - Greek - I John 5:8.) "The Lord God hath sent me, and His spirit. Thus saith the Lord, thy redeemer, the Holy one of Israel. - Isa. 48:16, 17. God's Spirit is not separate from Himself. Some one has said: "God the Father is that manifestation of God who is on the throne of the universe. God the Holy Ghost is that manifestation of the same Spirit everywhere present. Jesus Christ is that manifestation of the same Spirit who takes on a visible appearance." Man was made in the image of God, spirit, soul, and body.

The theme of the O. T. is one God. "Hear, O Israel, the Lord our God is one Lord." - Deut. 6:4.

Saul was addressing the Jehovah of his fathers, on the way to Damascus. "Who are Thou, Lord?" He did not know that God was "manifest in the flesh." Hear the Lord's own testimony and answer: "I am Jesus." - Acts 9:4, 5. That knocked Saul out. "In that day shall the Lord be one, and His name one." - Zech. 14-5, 9. To the Jews Jesus said: "Except ye believe that I am, ye shall die in your sins." - John 8:24. The whole purpose of God in the O. T. was to inculcate the idea of one God. This the Jews, after the Babylonian Captivity, which they suffered for their idolatry, never got away from. The "mystery of godliness," is the Incarnation. "God in Christ."

Those who deny that Jesus Christ is God, the absolute Deity, Deity the alone revelation and manifestation of the Father, are in line for the great Apostasy. Antichrist is battering at the walls of the church for a breach in the absolute Deity of the Lord Jesus Christ. If God can be known apart from Jesus Christ, or as a separate Person or Being from Jesus Christ, then we are bound to throw down the walls and embrace these anti-christian forces in one universal Fatherhood of God. And there must be two Gods, or Jesus Christ is not God. But Jesus Christ is God. There is no other saving manifestation of God. - Acts 4:12.

Spiritualists, Theosophists, Christian Scientists, etc., claim a knowledge of God outside of Christ. "Ye know neither me nor my Father. If ye knew me ye would know my Father also." - John 8:19. "Neither knoweth any man the Father, save the Son, and he to whomsoever the Son will reveal Him." - Matt. 11:27. Jesus is the full and only revelation of God to man.

The more we come to know Jesus in the Spirit the fuller revelation we receive of His Deity. "No man can say Jesus is Lord but by the Holy Ghost." - I Cor. 12:3. At first we see Him as our Mediator, our Sacrifice and Intercessor. Later we come to realize His absolute Deity, Godhead, oneness with the Father in essential being. Not simply oneness in accord. That is but a human proposition. He is both the Son of God, and God. - Luke 1:35, " Christ is the visible representation of the invisible God," - Col. 1:15-19, Weymouth. "For it is in Christ that the fullness of God's nature dwells embodied, and in Him ye are made complete." - Col. 2:9, 10, Weymouth. He is the "primal source" of all creatures." - Col 1:15, Worrell. Eph. 1:10, 17.

Draw a circle. Jesus is both our center and circumference. The simple minded cannot possibly go astray when they make Jesus everything. It is all in Jesus. Does He not satisfy us fully? If so, why seek another God beside Him? Outside of that circle we line up with Christian Scientists, Spiritualists, Theosophists, and every other anti-christian spirit.

Jesus is the first and last letter, the Alpha and Omega, from Genesis to Revelation. - Rev. 1:8, 17. Jesus is Emmanu-El, - Matt. 1:23. God incarnate is the mystery that confounds the false systems of religion. He is "all and in all." - Eph. 1:23, Col 3:11, Zech. 14:5-9.

We cannot find God outside of the Word. Jesus is the Word. Matt. 19:17; Mark 2:7-10; 4:41, Luke 5:21; 7:49; 8:25, John 6:64; 10:33; 12:45; 18:6, I Cor. 10:4; 9, Jas. 5:4 , 7, II Thess. 1:7-10, Rev. 1:12-17; 22:12, 13, Job 19:25-27, Ps. 50:1-7, Isa. 40:9, 10; 35:4; 59:15-20; 66:15, Dan. 7:13, 14.

"The Lord is my shepherd." - Ps. 23:1. "I am the good shepherd." - John 10:11. "He maketh me to lie down in green pastures." - Ps. 23:2. "Come unto me . . . I will give you rest." - Matt. 11:28. "He leadeth me in the paths of righteous." - Ps. 23:3 (Jer. 23:6). "But of Him are ye in Christ Jesus, who was made unto us righteousness." - I Cor. 1:30.

The power is in Jesus' name. Study Book of Acts and Epistles on this point. Matt. 10:22,

Mark 16:17, Luke 24:47, Acts 4:12; 15:14, etc., Eph. 1:21, Phil, 2:9, 10, Col. 3:17, I Peter 4:14, III John 7, Rev. 3:8, Heb. 13:15, Jas. 2:7 (Lev. 24:11), I Chron. 13:6, Deut. 28:58, Ex. 23:20, 21.

The subject of the Trinity is kaleidoscopic. The "persons" of the Godhead are like a dissolving view. One fades into another in true vision so perfectly and naturally that we cannot separate them. Yet God is not a mere Monad. The idea of God embraces Father, Son and Holy Spirit, a compound Personality. God showed me this figure in spiritual vision, all unsought for. It was repeated several times, at intervals of days, Father, Son and Holy Ghost continually resolved themselves into one, as in a dissolving view. I could not separate them. There was one God, one Substance. Nor could I tell one from the other.

All antichrist religions teach that Jesus was not absolute Deity. We could wish that the formers of the Nicean and Athanasian Creed had preserved the clear and powerful Apostolic vision of "God in Christ" that the early church possessed, instead of substituting "Greek Mysteries." The church had already fallen, the Roman Emperor Constantine himself calling the Nicean Council, presiding over its deliberations and punishing those daring to reject its decisions. This is a fact of history. He was a shrewd diplomat and politician. It is far better to "let the lid stay on the Ark" (Jesus is the Ark), than to delve into Greek mysteries. - (I Sam'l 6:19, Col. 2:9, 10.) God has gathered Himself up, concentrated Himself, visualized Himself in the person of Christ, that we might be able to approach and to know Him. - I John 5:20.

As men we understand man. We have no understanding of the animal kingdom. They have not our nature. Much less could we understand God except He had taken on Him our nature. God is God. Like Himself only. No other like Him. In the God-man, Jesus Christ, we understand Him. We do not even understand angels. Jesus is the "form" of God. - Phil. 2:6. The "form" is His nature, attributes and character. "God is Spirit." Jesus is the alone revelation of God. The Father refers us to Jesus. The Holy Ghost shines the light upon Jesus. He takes of the things of Christ and shows them to us. - John 16:12-14. The triune God is incarnate in Jesus. "For Christ is the very incarnation of the invisible God." - Col. 1:15, 20th Century Trans., Col. 2:9, 10. Jesus reveals the Father. John 14:6-11, 20; 10:30, Matt. 11:27. The Holy Ghost is the Spirit of the Father and the Son. - John 16:14. The Fatherhood, the Sonship, and the Eternal Spirit, are all manifest in Jesus Christ. He is the "eternal life." He is "the Spirit." - II Cor. 3:17, 18 (R. V.) There are three eternal distinctions in the Substance of God, but one Substance. The triune God, through the Incarnation, is united in humanity, for the salvation of man. - John 16:14 Heb. 2:16. "God manifest in the' flesh." The only revelation of God in the O. T. or the N. T. is Jesus Christ. He is the Theme of the Bible. Jesus is the "Word of God."

I once thought that Jesus loved the world, but that God hated us. Now I know that "God so loved the world." - John 3:16. It was God's love that saved us. As a child I feared my father. He did not seem to love me. But mother was tender, and loved me. She became my mediator with my father when he was angry at me. Just so I thought of the heavenly Father until I got a revelation of the real meaning of John 3:16. I found that God loved me. Jesus is the revelation of that love. They are one in love and sacrifice, offering for our salvation.

"The Son quickeneth whom he will." John 5:21. "The Father hath give all judgment unto the Son." - John 5:22. "That all may honor the Son even as they honor the Father." - John 5:23 (Greek). "The Father gave to the Son also to have life in himself." - John 5:26. "I (Jesus) will raise him up at the last day." - John 6:40, 44, 54. "I have power to lay down my life - and to take it again." - John 10:18. "I give unto them eternal life." - John 10:28. I am the resurrection and the life." - John 11:25, I Cor. 15:45. The Father raises Jesus from the dead. - Rom 6:4. The Spirit raises Jesus from the dead. - Rom 8:11. Jesus raises himself from the dead. - John 10:17, 18.

Father and Son are one in a much deeper sense than mere agreement in action. They are inherently one in essential being. This is a much deeper oneness than that of husband and wife, or of even Christ and the church, which is His "body." "These three are one." - I John 5:7, "the only born God." V. L. "an only begotten God.´- Rotherham. - John 10:17, 18.

The "Word" returns to the "bosom of the Father." - John 1:18; 16:28. It carries with it the glorified humanity of Jesus Christ, the incarnation "bodily." He is the "temple of God." He dwells in the glory, and the glory dwells in Him. - I Tim 6:16. "And the city hath no need of the sun, for the glory of God did lighten it, and the lamp thereof is the Lamb." - Rev. 21:23. The Lamb is the lamp that the light of God shines through. The light is softened for our approach in Jesus Christ. He is both the sheep-fold and the Shepherd, the High Priest and the offering. As High Priest He offers Himself. He is both God and the Son of God. How this can all be reason may never explain, but the Word of God declares it. His reward is with Him. - Rev. 22:12. He shall feed His flock like a shepherd. - Isa. 40:9-11, John 10. This is Jesus Christ the Rewarder, and Good Shepherd. It is impossible to exalt Him too highly. The one God is so constituted and contained in the Lord Jesus Christ as to absolutely prohibit any other God. The world must accept Jesus Christ as their God. The world is being rapidly prepared to accept the Antichrist as God. The apostasy of the church is paving the way for this by denying the Deity of Jesus Christ. Which side shall we be found on? "If another shall come in his own name, him ye will receive." - John 5:43.

Thank God we have an unqualified Christ. He is neither qualified as to His Being or His power. He has "all power." - Matt 28:18. He is "the Alpha and Omega, the Beginning and the End: the First and the Last." There is none before nor after Him. He is "the Mighty God." - Isa. 9:6. He is "all and in all." We may well fear any teaching or people who show a tendency to minimize or deny either the power or Personality of Jesus Christ."

"Who is the image of the invisible God." - Col. 1:15. "Now unto the king eternal, incorruptible, invisible." - I Tim. 1:17; Isa. 9:66:16. "Thou hast magnified thy word above all thy name." - Ps. 138:2. Jesus is the Word - "For in Him all the fulness of the Godhead was pleased to dwell." - Col. 1:19, Scofield. Jesus is "all the fulness," and "fills all." - Eph. 1:23, John 1:16. We know Christ "after the flesh" no more." - II Cor. 5:16. No man knows anything of the "form" or nature, character or attributes of God except in Jesus Christ. Who is it the world is rejecting, and always has rejected? Jesus.

"That in the ages to come He might show the exceeding riches of His grace in kindness toward us in Christ Jesus." - Eph. 2:7. Throughout the countless ages of eternity we shall not be able to fathom fully the lengths and breadths and depths and heights of God in Christ. - Eph. 3:18. Do we need a revelation of God outside of Christ? Then we must seek for another plan of salvation. But we are "complete in Him." "God is Spirit." He is Omnipresent, everywhere. We cannot see Spirit. We are creatures, created beings, not as God - Deut. 4:12-16. Jesus is the visible of the invisible. We shall surely not be disappointed in seeing God in Him. Jesus Christ is the plan of salvation." He is the revelation of the Father, the channel of the Holy Ghost, "God manifest in the flesh," the fulness of the Godhead bodily." Those who are expecting to know and see God apart from Jesus Christ stand in grave danger of being disappointed in Him. They do not know Christ fully. "These three are one." Jesus is the one to fill our vision. He will do it completely. The Holy Ghost reveals not Himself, but Christ. He is the Spirit of the glorified Christ. He is a great light, reflected on Christ. - John 16:14. "I am in the Father and the Father in me." - John 14:11. "For ye are dead, and your life is hid with Christ in God" - Col. 3:3. Who is it the world must meet some day in judgment? Jesus. John 5:22, Rom. 14:10.

Adam heard God in the "wind of the day" (margin). - Gen 3:8. "The wind bloweth where it listeth and thou hearest the voice thereof ." - John 3:8. Jesus was the Word. Job cries, "I know that my redeemer liveth, and that he shall stand up at the last upon the earth. In my flesh shall I see God." - Job 19:25, 26. Jesus Christ is "God our Savior." - Titus 1:3. Only God can reveal God. - I Cor. 2:11.

God "tabernacled" in Jesus Christ. The Word that "was God," "tabernacled among us." - John 1:14. "God created man in His own image." - Gen 1:27. One image. Peter would have also built three tabernacles. There is one tabernacle, Jesus Christ. See "Jesus only." John 2:19-21. Jesus was the "express image" of the "invisible God." - Heb. 1:3, Col. 1:15.

Adam was the father of the race naturally. Jesus became the Father of the race spiritually, the "second Adam." He is the revelation of the Father. God becomes our Father in Christ. The Sonship reveals the Fatherhood. And we become sons thereby. Deity has no father. Jesus is absolute Deity for Deity is His real Personality. Only His human nature was "begotten" in the womb of Mary. - Luke 1:35, Rotherham. God is spoken of in Heb. 12:9, as "the father of spirits." Adam got his spirit direct from God. But Jesus' real Personality was God.

The "life which was with the Father" Was manifested in Jesus Christ. - I John 1:2. He is the "eternal life." - I John 5:20. He has "life in Himself." - John 5:26. Through revelation of Jesus Christ." - Gal. 1:12. "Of Him are ye in Christ Jesus." - I Cor. 1:30. The treasures of wisdom and knowledge are hidden in Christ." - Col. 2:3. The mystery of His will is purposed in Christ." - Eph. 1:19. The "finished work of Calvary" and the "Godhead" question simply resolve themselves into salvation and the manifestation of God in Jesus Christ alone.

The disciples understood God aright. All there is for us of God is found in Jesus. This does not deny the Father. The Book of Acts gives us the position in which they held Jesus, and the power they realized in His name. That was the secret of their ministry and success. They knew Jesus as "the Mighty God," the fact the Antichrist and the Apostasy deny. All there is for us of God is in that Name - Jesus. The disciples rejoiced to be counted worthy to "suffer dishonor for the Name." - Acts 5:41, I Peter 4:14, 16.

When we really know Jesus as "the Mighty God" we may also "do exploits." - Dan. 11:32. We must know God in Christ, through the Eternal Spirit. We must know Jesus as "both Lord and Christ," and the power in His Name. - Acts 2:36. "He is Lord of all." - Acts 10:36. "The Lord is the Spirit." - II Cor. 3:17. In Acts 16:6, 7, R. V., the Holy Ghost and Spirit of Christ are used interchangeably. See Acts 5:3, 4, 9. "the supply of the Spirit of Jesus Christ." - Phil. 1:19. The Word and Person who utters it are not separated. My thought and speech are essentially myself.

Jesus was Himself "the beginning and the ending." - Rev. 1:8, 17. The beginning of all God's self-revelation is found in Christ. He is both the Alpha and the Omega. "Jehovah" (Jesus) signifies the God that was, is, and will be. "Jesus Christ the same yesterday, and today, and forever." - Heb. 13:8.

In His humanity, union with man, Jesus was distinct from and inferior to the Father, and must of necessity speak of Himself as such. Mary would have touched His humanity. He spoke to her as a man. - John 20:17. He was to be revealed to them in His Deity. The disciples had only known Him heretofore as a man. In Mexico the Roman Catholics worship three Gods, in separate, corporeal forms. They have a picture of this idea, which they worship. But if Christ is "all and in all" why do we look for more than all?

In Rev 5, a lamb takes the book. But Jesus is not a literal lamb. This is figurative speech. Dan. 7:1, 13, - This is a vision, not a literal scene. "The worlds were framed by the word of God." - Heb. 11:3. This Word was Jesus. The Word did all the speaking in the revelation of God. The Word in heaven testifies to the Son on earth. The Word is omnipresent, and eternal. - I John 5:7. The Bible speaks of three in one, but never of one in three. Jesus is "at the right hand of God," spiritually, the place of power. - Matt. 26:64. He is "in God." - Col. 3:3. "God is Spirit." And the Father God is in Christ, "all the fulness of the Godhead," and we are "complete in Him." - Col. 2:9, 10. He is all there is of God for us. Do we really know Jesus? He is "all and in all."

The Jesus returned to His disciples as "another Comforter." - John 14:16, 18. He was the same Christ, but no longer "in the flesh." They were to know Him now in a higher sense. Jesus has been with them, but He is to be in them. "In that day ye shall know that I am in my Father and ye in me, and I in you" - John 14:20, 26, 16:12-14. This was on the day of Pentecost when the "other Comforter" came. "Christ in you the hope of glory" - Col. 1:27. He is the Eternal Spirit, the eternal life." "The Spirit was not yet given because Jesus was not yet glorified." - John John 7:39. Jesus had been with the disciples and was about to leave them. Their hearts were sad. What would they do without Him? They did not want another. Hence His words, "I will not leave you orphans (Greek), I will come unto you," be a Father to you. - John 14:18. He was going away that He might come closer, be in them, through the Holy Ghost, forever. "And lo I am with you alway, even unto the end of the world. - Matt. 28:20. They are to know Jesus "after the flesh" no more. - II Cor. 5:16.

Jesus does not simply represent God. He is God. We do not say that He is the Father. But He is the manifestation and the revelation of the Father to us. The Father is in Him, for us. It is impossible to make too much of the Lord Jesus Christ. He is everything to us, and all we need. The Son of God is the Father's "fellow," human form. - Zech. 13:7. The dispensation of the Father is in the Son. He dispenses Himself to us in the Son. Jesus taught us to pray, "Our Father." "He that confesseth the Son hath the Father also." - I John 2:23. "He that abideth in the teaching, the same hath both the Father and the Son." - II John 9. "I am the way, and the truth, and the life; no one cometh unto the Father, but by me." - John 14:6. "I am the resurrection and the life." - John 11:25. "God was in Christ reconciling the world unto Himself." - II Cor. 5:19. "Even as God also in Christ forgave you." - Eph 4:32. "That ye may know the mystery of God, Christ." - Col. 2:2. "God was manifest in the flesh." - I Tim. 3:16. No one can have the Son without the Father. And no one can have the Father without the Son.

I have never felt, when preaching that Jesus is God, that the Father was in any sense neglected, denied, or displeased. In fact, I have always felt that He was mightily pleased. I have never been conscious of denying Him. I have often asked Him to help me to exalt Jesus more. I am so weak and unable, either in understanding or example, to do so. But I have never been so blessed in my soul as when doing so. And the Holy Ghost always wonderfully helps me. In fact I had never heard until the last few years, since the Apostasy has set in, that it was possible to exalt Jesus Christ too highly. We did not use to think that way about it.

I confess I am becoming more and more afraid at the possibility of throwing my sympathy on the wrong side, my influence in the wrong direction, against Christ. I cannot afford in any sense or degree to sympathize, take sides with, or aid the Antichrist. I am afraid of the spirit of apostasy. The Pentecostal people stand at the parting of the ways on this question. Will they also help prepare the way for the Antichrist? It is a solemn issue. It is Christ or Antichrist. Are we going to gradually surrender our Lord to the enemy to be crucified, also? We declare in all seriousness many are already doing so.

The spirit of Antichrist (against Christ), the apostasy, is gradually, subtly, but surely, creeping over the Pentecostal people. Of this we have abundant evidence. It is going to become harder and harder to preach the absolute Deity of Christ. This is a terrible thing. Many of our people are already fast becoming Higher Critics, along many lines, denying the Deity of Christ, and the inspiration of the whole Bible. The apostasy has struck the Pentecostal Movement. Have we any reason to believe that we shall be spared this more than others? History repeats itself. We are the same as others, only more privileged. We have more to answer for.

This is not a mere matter of "old issue" or "new issue," so-called. If we fail to confess and preach the absolute Deity of Christ we are yielding to the Antichrist. No matter how many may have overshot the mark, God has a controversy with His people. Dare we through fear of being "numbered among transgressors" deny our Eternal Lord? The devil is shutting many a mouth through fear today. As the Sun frequently appears oblong at its rising, through refraction of its rays, because of abnormal, unfavorable, atmospheric conditions, so with the present issue. The truth is hindered and distorted by our human misconceptions, wounded in the house of its friends.

Jesus Christ being robbed of His Deity today. That is the real issue. No matter what others may have done, how they may have abused the truth, through ignorance, etc., will we deny our Lord? It is better to even overexalt Him, if such a thing were possible, through honest ignorance, than to deny Him. God will accept the one, where the heart motive is pure, through misunderstanding, but reject the other. It is not a human issue. Our wrestling is not "with flesh and blood." "Lord, what shall this man do? What is that to thee; follow thou me." We shall answer each for himself in the matter.

God will not reveal Himself to "party spirit." We must be cleansed from this evil also. He cannot reveal Himself to men in carnal conflict. Jesus is again "crucified between two thieves," between two selfish "party" extremes. Both are robbing Him. We need a fuller, clearer revelation of the Deity of Christ. We must have God's issue, the balanced truth, without fear or favor, ignorance or prejudice. Extremes can only hope to meet in Christ, in the middle.

Philip Schaff, D. D.; LL. D., has said: "The divisions of Christendom will be overruled at last for a deeper and richer harmony, of which Christ is the key-note. In Him and by Him all problems of theology and history will be solved.

In the best case a human creed is only an approximate and relatively correct exposition of revealed truth, and may be improved by the progressive knowledge of the Church, while the Bible remains perfect and infallible. Any higher view of the authority of Creeds is unprotestant and essentially Romanizing."

Let us pray God that this may soon be realized. Some one has said, "Believers hate each other more for the things they disagree upon, than they love one another for the things in which they do agree." This is a sad situation. The reformers in Luther's and Zwingle's day, when the Protestants of Germany and Switzerland came together to see if they could come to any possible agreement, and thus be enabled to stand together against their common foe, the terrible Roman hierarchy, were surprised to find how many things they really did agree upon. If we would seek today to see how many things we are agreed upon, rather than to see how many we can disagree upon, and thus separate, scatter and divide our strength and the "body," we might really be surprised and joyed at our findings.

We confess to a very limited capacity for handling such a profound subject, and crave the charity and leniency of all in their judgment of this contribution. Jesus said of Mary, "She hath done what she could." - (Mark 14:6-8.) We have given, for the most part, the testimony of others in the matter. We wish to claim authority over no man's conscience. May the Lord be merciful to us all, further illuminating our minds and understanding in the knowledge of Him. We "know in part" only, at the best. - I Cor. 13:9. In humility let us together seek His face for further grace and favor. And wherein we may have erred may we be forgiven.

"All hail the power of Jesus' Name, let angels prostrate fall; Bring forth the royal diadem, and crown Him Lord of all."

CHAPTER VI

DOUBTLESS the reader will expect to find something at least in this book on the "Baptismal Formula" question. With Paul, we have never felt that were sent to baptize, but "to preach the Gospel." We have never personally baptized anyone in our ministry. We believe the vital point is for converts to understand clearly the plan of salvation, and to give a clear witness to the world that they have accepted, taken upon them the name of, and been discipled to, the Lord Jesus Christ. But we will give the arguments on the subject for consideration. Possibly we are in as much danger of becoming formulists as we are of becoming formalists.

In "The Truth about the Godhead," published by the General Council, Assemblies of God, by E. N. Bell, we read "Those early christians did not hold slavishly to the words in Matt. 28:19, as a fixed law, as they would have done had they understood Jesus to prescribe an unvarying formula, a law. If they (the saints of today) held Matt. 28:19 was all right, but not the only form; if they merely held that other forms were acceptable, and did not purposely and wilfully oppose mention of the Father and the Holy Ghost, then they would be in respectable, scholarly company, for Hastings Dictionary of the Bible says at top of page 241, Vol. I, "That in the Apostolic Age there was no fixed formula is shown not only by the difference between Matthew and Acts, but by the difference between one passage in Acts and others in Acts itself, and also by traces of other differences (variations) in the Epistles.

"The shorter forms (Acts) have been sometimes used in the Pentecostal Movement from the beginning without any opposition to Matt. 28:19, and without having any special doctrinal reason for using the shorter forms. So long as this was the custom no issue was raised. Either way was regarded as acceptable." - E. N. Bell, for General Council. This we know to be true. Some very prominent leaders, now in the Council, baptized in the name of the Lord "Jesus Christ."

In the Encyclopedia Brittanica we read: "Name stands for personality in the N. T. The likeness of the baptismal ceremony with Christ's death and resurrection insured a real union with Him of the believer, according to Paul. The Apostolic age supplied this identification, and the normal mode of baptism during it seems to have been, "Into Christ Jesus, etc." As a rule the repentant underwent baptism in the name of Christ Jesus, and washed away their sins before hands were laid upon them unto the reception of the Spirit.

"Eusebius Pamphili, in nearly a score of citations, substitutes the words "in My Name," for the words "baptizing them into the name of the Father, and of the Son, and of the Holy Ghost." The first Gospel (Matt.) thus falls into line with the rest of the N. T." - Ency. Britt.

We have simply quoted what we find in history. There are many other statements to the same effect, proving conclusively that "baptism in Jesus' name" was at least extensively practiced in the first centuries of the church. We cannot change Church History.

In the enlarged Nicene Creed, Constantinople Council, A. D., 381, we read "We acknowledge one baptism for the remission of sins," (Acts 2:38, Luke24:47).

In the Greek Church Catechism, A. D., 1829, we read "What is required of him that seeks to be baptized? - Ans. - Repentance and faith: for which cause, also before baptism they recite the Creed, "Repent and be baptized everyone of you in the name of Jesus Christ for the remission of sins, and ye shall receive the gift of the Holy Ghost." - (Acts 2:38.)

Rev. Geo. Candel, Toledo, Ohio, in 1907 wrote: "Now if any rule of faith and practice could be formulated from these examples (of baptism in Acts) it might be this: that baptism into the name of Jesus should be urged as a fitting fruit of repentance, and as a condition of receiving forgiveness and the gift of the Spirit, to Jews or to other people who have indulged in any special hatred of Jesus or opposition to Him as the divine Savior. Consenting to this requirement, in such a case, would be necessary to a thorough repentance." (In that case, would not most people need to be baptized that way today, for growing spirit of antichrist is sweeping all ranks, both religious and secular.) The Gentiles at Cornelius' household were also baptized "in the name of Jesus Christ." - R. V., Acts 10:48.

Dr. R. A. Torrey, in his book entitled "What the Bible Teaches," has written as follows: "In a normal state of the church every believer would have the baptism with the Holy Spirit as in the church at Corinth. - I Cor. 12:13. In such a normal state of the church the baptism with the Holy

Spirit would be received immediately upon repentance and baptism into the name of Jesus Christ for the remission of sins - Acts 2:38." Whatever the writer meant by this it stands thus written.

"Baptized into what name?" This question was asked of the editor of the Sunday School Times by a Sunday School Union Worker. The Sunday School Times has a list of over one hundred thousand subscribers and enters the homes of almost that many members of different churches all over the Union. We give the Editor's reply: "The name of Jesus carries with it all the power of the triune God, for "in Him dwelleth all the fullness of the Godhead bodily" (Col. 2:9). His disciples' request that He show them the Father brought from Jesus the startlingly definite reply: "He that hath seen me hath seen the Father" (John 14:9). When John in the Revelation prophesied, They shall see His face; and His name shall be on their foreheads' (Rev. 22:4), that name and that face revealed God in all His fullness, and doubtless are the name and face of Jesus, when we shall see Him as He is.'

It may well be, therefore, that the disciples in baptizing in the name of Jesus were carrying out the commission of Matt. 28:19. In both cases there is one God and one Name. Some Christians who have felt that the spiritual reality was not in the form of baptism that they received have had the ordinance performed again and received rich blessing through it. Certainly either form is a true baptism if the reality is back of the ceremony. Yet there seems no reason for urging a second ceremony on the ground of this difference in the formula." - Sunday School Times.

Another writer, not Pentecostal, has said: While the matter is expressed in detail in Matt. 28:19, yet in Jesus "dwelleth all the fullness of the Godhead bodily, and ye are complete in Him. - Col. 2:9, 10. In Jesus was the Father's name or character, and the fulness of the Spirit. Therefore when the Apostles baptized "into Jesus' name," they carried out our Lord's injunction. - (Matt. 28:19.)

Many have admitted that if it were not for Matt. 28:19, the logical way, in view of the other Scriptures, especially Acts, would be to baptize, "in Jesus' name." Salvation is in "no other name." - Act 4:12, Luke 24:47. We do everything else in Jesus' name. - Mark 16. "At the mouth of two or three witnesses." - II Cor. 13:1. This is God's rule. There are several to the name of Jesus. "Were ye baptized into the name of Paul?" "Were ye baptized into the name of Paul?" - I Cor. 1:13. This would seem to imply that they should be baptized into the name of the one to whom they were disciplined. How else could they confess Christ?

We have given the general arguments used in favor of Acts 2:38, etc. The arguments for Matt. 28:19, are too well known to require repetition. We are honest truth seekers. None but fools would seek to change the Word of God.

In "One hundred Contradictions of the Bible," a little book extensively circulated among all unbelievers, the seeming discrepancy between Matt.28:19, and Acts 2:38, is cited as a contradiction. What a pity that believers Cannot find the secret of the agreement between these two Scriptures, and thus present solid front to stop the mouths of the infidels and enemies of their common Lord and Master, instead of fighting one another, each with half the truth, thus confirming unbelievers in their infidelity. We shall have to answer to God for this failure. "That they all may be one: that the world may believe." - John 17:21.

We that God's Word is not a Chinese Puzzle. There must be an explanation somewhere. And nothing is ever really settled until it is settled right. So far the brethren have been largely fighting one another, each with of the truth against the, or ignoring, if not denying, a part of the truth altogether. This is bad business. We dare not question the inspiration of the inspiration of the whole Word of God.

When the writer was baptized in the Baptist church, 30 years ago, he received the impression that the preacher was baptizing him by the authority (in the name) of the Father, Son and Holy Ghost. The commission of Matt. 28:19, was pre-Pentecostal. Jesus at that time had many things to say to them, but they could not bear them yet. - John 16:12, 13. When the Holy Ghost, "the Spirit of truth," should be come, at Pentecost, He would "guide them into all truth." One of these truths was certainly "the mystery of godliness," hidden from the ages, the fulness or Deity in Jesus Christ, our completeness in Him, and salvation in His name. - Acts 4:12. That these truths were not really understood or realized by the disciples before the Holy Ghost was given, I think all will agree. They could not have understood them. "The Spirit was not yet given, for Jesus was not yet glorified." Jesus could not come in the Spirit until He had left them in the body. They were not yet "born again," in the N. T. sense of the word. Their experience was dispensational. In N. T. order they seem to have received the new birth and the baptism with the Holy Ghost as but two parts of one normal whole. This was a normal N. T. experience. They believed, were baptized in water, and received the Holy Ghost.

Some have already adopted some such order in the baptismal formula as we have suggested above, but unfortunately, for some reason have placed the cart before the horse in the matter. Matt. 28:19, comes first, the Book of Acts order later, in process of revelation, unfolding and action.

The Deity of Christ

Yet we do not profess to have fully solved the situation. In Matt. 28:19, our Authorized Version reads, "in the name." The Revised Version gives it, "into the name." While the Greek renders it, "to the name." In the Book of Acts we meet with the same difficulty, the Authorized and R. V. versions differing there also. In some cases it is rendered "in," in other cases "into," these versions differing on the same passages. In the Greek the prepositions used vary in the different cases, in some places the word being rendered "in," in other cases "to." The same Greek word "to," in Matt. 28:19, is used in two instances in the Book of Acts (8:16; 19:5), to the name of the Lord Jesus Christ." In the Syriac Version, one of the oldest and most authentic in existence, the translation is simply "in" in every case. These things being true we should certainly have charity at least with one another.

We understand that in the Pentecostal work in Canada the brethren graciously allow full liberty of conscience in this matter, and still fellowship one another fully. This would seem to be, under the circumstances, the only real sane and christian procedure. If Pentecostal saints cannot have at least this much tolerance in religion we are surely little better than the papists after all. Brethren, let us pray for one another.

Los Angeles. California
March, 1926

www.ingramcontent.com/pod-product-compliance
Lightning Source LLC
Chambersburg PA
CBHW022032090426
42739CB00006BA/388